CALLED
BY
GOD

The Bible Reading Fellowship
15 The Chambers, Vineyard
Abingdon OX14 3FE
brf.org.uk

The Bible Reading Fellowship (BRF) is a Registered Charity (233280)

ISBN 978 0 85746 530 6
First published 2017
10 9 8 7 6 5 4 3 2 1 0
All rights reserved

Acknowledgements
Unless otherwise stated, scripture quotations are taken from The Holy Bible, New International
Version (Anglicised edition) copyright © 1979, 1984, 2011 by Biblica. Used by permission of
Hodder & Stoughton Publishers, an Hachette UK company. All rights reserved. 'NIV' is a registered
trademark of Biblica. UK trademark number 1448790.

Scripture quotations from The New Revised Standard Version of the Bible, Anglicised edition,
copyright © 1989, 1995 by the Division of Christian Education of the National Council of the
Churches of Christ in the United States of America. Used by permission. All rights reserved.

Every effort has been made to trace and contact copyright owners for material used in this
resource. We apologise for any inadvertent omissions or errors, and would ask those concerned
to contact us so that full acknowledgement can be made in the future.

A catalogue record for this book is available from the British Library

Printed and bound by CPI Group (UK) Ltd, Croydon CR0 4YY

CALLED
BY
GOD

EXPLORING OUR
IDENTITY IN CHRIST

DEREK TIDBALL

BRF

To my wonderful wife

Dianne

on the occasion of her serving as
President of the Baptist Union of Great Britain
2017–18

Contents

Introduction

More than once in the New Testament Christians are described as 'the called ones' (Romans 1:1, 6, 7; 1 Corinthians 1:2, 24). It is plain that being called by God was not reserved for a special elite group of Christians but applied to every Christian. The call of God determined their identity in Christ. But what exactly does it mean to be called by God?

One of the greatest achievements of the Reformation was the rethinking of 'the call'. During the Middle Ages it had been thought that vocation—the word comes from the Latin word for 'to call'—was the province of priests and monks. Their spiritual work and contemplative lives were on a different plane from that of ordinary workers, like farmers, traders and servants. Religious professionals needed a call and had a vocation; the rest just had work. Martin Luther began to liberate the concept of the call from the monopoly hold of the clergy and re-envision all work, however ordinary, as significant in God's sight and a calling from him. This holistic vision was much more in line with the teaching of scripture than the previous distorted views of vocation had been (see, for example, Colossians 3:18—4:1).

Reformation teaching on vocation had a great and lasting impact but did not produce a totally satisfactory result. Having escaped the confinement of the religious specialists, other particular occupations or professions came to be seen as vocations. These were still often deemed more worthy than mundane work, especially if they involved long hours, low pay and other elements of self-sacrifice. What is more, in the Protestant church, as well as the Roman Catholic Church, our language still suggests that those who become ministers, missionaries or full-time Christian workers are the ones we truly consider to have (and need) a call, as opposed to those who are accountants, engineers, shelf-stackers or builders. Nevertheless, though the Reformation may not have achieved a perfect result in this area, it was a giant leap forward.

Much current discussion is about work and, indeed, about viewing the whole of life as a calling, and rightly so.[1] I endorse the importance of such discussions. We have a long way to go still in casting the biblical vision that life in its totality, and one's work in particular, however apparently secular, is a calling from God. The curious thing in all this, however, is how little attention is paid to what the Bible sets out as the Christian's calling. On numerous occasions the New Testament, building on an Old Testament theme, says not only that Christians are 'the called ones' but also that they are called to this or called to that. The purpose of this book is to reflect on the major texts that articulate the biblical vision of what it means to be called by God, and so to explore our identity in Christ.

After an opening chapter, which lays an important foundation, the book is roughly organised around the phases of the Christian life from the initial calling heard in conversion to what the Salvation Army speaks of as 'being promoted to glory'. It's not as neat as that, of course, since many of the texts considered refer to simultaneous experiences in our journey as Christians. There is some inevitable overlap between the chapters but they are designed to stand alone. Each chapter concludes with a one- or two-sentence 'Key lesson' and a short list of questions for group discussion or personal consideration.

If you are looking for something to help you see your job as a vocation, there would be better books to read than this one. But if you want to anchor your understanding in what the Bible explicitly says about the Christian's calling, which inevitably has major implications for the whole of our lives, this may be the place to start. Without such an anchor it's too easy to drift in the sea of our own changing opinions. This will give us a solid fixed point on which to reflect on God's calling to us today.

I

Called… loved… kept

To those who have been called, who are loved in God the Father and kept for Jesus Christ.
JUDE 1

One of the most important foundations of the Christian life is that you are called to it. I know this is different from the popular idea of what happens when people become Christians. When we tell our stories we often say, 'I decided to follow Jesus' or 'I committed my life to Christ', or perhaps we talk of 'finding faith' with 'I' as the unspoken explorer who has made the discovery. We live in a culture of individualism where 'I' is in danger of becoming the subject of every sentence. But to be called is to respond to the initiative of another and, having done so, to commence a life which will be profoundly reshaped, in the company of others who have also responded to the call.

The New Testament spells out a number of dimensions to this calling that together give a comprehensive account of the Christian life. Here we begin with one of its most inclusive claims.

Jude gives the most astonishing and unexpected beginning to his little and often-neglected letter, which we find tucked away at the back of our Bibles. The heart of the letter (vv. 3–16) is fierce in its denunciation of those who were destroying the church of his day. He tells us he had wanted to write a more positive letter, rejoicing in the salvation they shared. Yet the danger was such that he had to set that aside in order to warn the church to expel the ungodly people who had infiltrated it and were perverting the grace of God, just as we would want to destroy cancer cells that were fatally invading our body. He pronounces sure and certain judgement on them, in the most graphic of terms.

Perhaps it is precisely because of the harshness of his tone and the seriousness of his warning that his letter begins (and will end) so positively. His opening words radiate pastoral assurance. His readers are far from being a perfect church, yet the main body of members, as opposed to the infiltrators, can be assured that they are 'called… loved… and kept' (v. 1), three great words which define the Christian life. Furthermore, he wants them to know 'mercy, peace and love', not just a little but 'in abundance' (v. 2).

Great words. What do they mean?

Called

A word full of assurance

My hold on God is variable and often uncertain. It wouldn't be true to say it changes as often as the weather, but it is woefully affected by circumstances, moods and commitments. There are times when God feels so close and his blessing so real that he is almost tangible. At other times, especially when the challenges mount and when failure is experienced, my grip on him loosens. How great it is to know then that what really counts is not my grip on God but his calling of me.

God, 'who does not change like shifting shadows' (James 1:17) and isn't subject to the fluctuations we humans suffer, has issued the call. God, who never suffers from partial or imperfect knowledge, knew all there was to know about me, yet still called me into his family and service. God, who knows the end from the beginning, has elected me—that's inherent in his call—to be his servant. I may not think I qualify. I may not believe I am mature, gifted, good, stable, knowledgeable, zealous or wise enough, but it did not prevent him from calling.

As Alec Motyer once wrote:

Salvation would be a miserably unsure thing had it no other foundation than that I chose Christ. The human will blows hot and blows cold, is firm and unstable by fits and starts; it can offer no security of tenure. But the will of God is the ground of salvation.[2]

There can be no surer ground on which to stand than that the all-knowing and all-powerful God has called us to be his own.

Called for a purpose

From the beginning, God has been a calling God. Adam and Eve were given the special calling to act as God's representatives on earth, ruling as wise stewards over the natural creation and propagating the human race (Genesis 1:28). Sadly, their desire to become 'like God' himself (3:4) fatally infected their original calling and from then on Adam and Eve were estranged from God with lasting consequences for their heirs. Hence, on the evening of the day on which they disobeyed God, he called Adam asking, 'Where are you?'(3:9).

In spite of this disastrous start, God did not give up calling. He continued to seek people who could both become his friends and serve him as his agents of blessing in the world. Outstanding in the long line of calls is the call he gave to Abraham: 'Go from your country, your people and your father's household to the land I will show you' (Genesis 12:1). It was courageous, or foolhardy, of Abraham to accept the call. I'm pretty sure I would have wanted to know more about the destination before I agreed to pack! Perhaps it was the sense of purpose that was inherent in the call that inspired Abraham to up sticks and go. The call—or election, by another name—was never intended for Abraham's private enjoyment or personal prosperity but was for the benefit of all peoples. It was so that he would be the father of a great nation through whom 'all peoples on earth will be blessed' (12:2–3). Now that's a calling! It's no small mission but is global in its reach. Just as with Adam and Eve, God's calling was for Abraham to be an instrument in his hand to bless others.

The children of Israel, on whom Abraham's election collectively devolved, occasionally fulfilled their calling well but, sadly, more often than not failed to live in accordance with their vocation. They presumed it meant that God would give them preferential treatment and bless them as a nation, providing them with protection and prosperity, irrespective of how they lived. So they frequently took liberties and lived in a way that offended the God who longed to care for them. Instead of being a channel of God's blessing to others they tried to keep it to themselves. The idea of calling and election became thoroughly distorted in their minds.

Yet God did not give up. He kept calling: shepherds, like Moses, to rescue them (Exodus 3:1—4:17); judges, like Gideon, to deliver them (Judges 6); priests, like Samuel, to guide them (1 Samuel 3); kings, like David, to rule them (1 Samuel 16:1–13); and above all prophets—many prophets—to call them to repentance and a new way of living (Isaiah 6; Jeremiah 1:4–19; Ezekiel 1—3; Amos 7:14–15).

It would be a mistake to think that God only called individual people, and an even greater mistake to think he only called exceptional people to act on his behalf in the world. His specific call may have focused on Joshua, Deborah, Isaiah or Huldah at a particular time, but Israel as a whole had received the call. As mentioned, the whole nation, not just a few representative leaders, had been called to be 'a kingdom of priests and a holy nation' (Exodus 19:6). It was a vocation they rarely understood, but one which was re-envisioned by the prophet Isaiah. Through him God reminded Israel:

I took you from the ends of the earth,
from its furthest corners I called you,
I said, 'You are my servant';
I have chosen you and have not rejected you.
ISAIAH 41:9

I, the Lord, have called *you in righteousness;*
I will take hold of your hand.
I will keep you and will make you
to be a covenant for the people
and a light for the Gentiles.
ISAIAH 42:6

Listen to me, Jacob,
Israel, whom I have called*:*
I am he;
I am the first and I am the last.
ISAIAH 48:12

Listen to me, you islands;
hear this, you distant nations:
before I was born the Lord called *me;*
from my mother's womb he has spoken my name…
He said to me, 'You are my servant,
Israel, in whom I will display my splendour.'
ISAIAH 49:1, 3 (ALL EMPHASES MINE)

It is against this background that Jude addresses his readers, and through them us, as those who are called. Jesus, of course, called the Twelve to be his apostles (Mark 3:13–19) and many others to follow him (for example, Matthew 9:9; 22:14). But Jude's concern is not with outstanding individuals but with the church as a whole, which has a long and distinguished pedigree as those who are called to serve God in the world by being his special and holy (more of that later) people and the means by which the gospel would bless the world. The calling of Israel has now been entrusted to the followers of Jesus Christ.

Calling implies responsibility and privilege

Calling, then, gives a sense of purpose and significance in life. We have a mission to fulfil. It prevents us from drifting through with no particular direction or destination in mind.

Although we speak in general conversation of being 'called' less than we did, we still speak of people as 'called to the bar' (that is, the legal, not the alcoholic, one) or being 'called up' into the armed services—a distant memory in the UK, perhaps, but a present experience for many young people in other countries. And while the managerialism of the present culture may have diluted the sense of vocation, the law, the armed forces, medicine and the police, among others, are still vocations that have the implications of calling about them.

These callings confer special rights and responsibilities that are denied ordinary people. Barristers who are called to the bar have a right of audience before judges in the higher courts which ordinary mortals do not have. Their training and testing has qualified them to practise law in a specialised way, and to wear the symbolic dress of gown and wig appropriate to their office. Being called up to fight in a war also involves rigorous training and with it the right to bear arms in the Queen's name as well as to wear the appropriate uniform. Without that, bearing arms would usually be a criminal offence. After years of training and the swearing of the Hippocratic oath, doctors are able to examine patients, dispense medicines, stick needles in people and authorise treatments which others would be in trouble for if they did. Nurses equally serve in a vocation, although many might feel the element of self-sacrifice and service outweighs any privileges their qualification entails. Police officers are called to swear an oath that they will uphold the Queen's law, with the result that they are held in some respect, if not awe (even if they feel this has been somewhat eroded in recent days), and given powers denied to members of the public. Each vocation involves observing certain ethical standards. Calling involves both responsibilities and rights.

Think in more everyday terms. When we receive an invitation to a wedding we are effectively being called to it. People go to great lengths to enjoy the privilege of being a guest. The date is kept free, a present is bought, the hair is done, and a new outfit is bought to wear, all so they have the privilege of being a guest. The invitation (call) confers responsibilities (not to turn up dressed like a tramp and to bring a present with you) and the right to attend the reception and eat the wedding breakfast (as it is oddly called).

How much more seriously we should take our calling to be Christians! And how much greater are the privileges that we enjoy. Our calling as Christians confers the responsibility of following Christ obediently, serving the living God in the world he has made and participating in the fulfilling of his purposes for it. It confers the right of being sons and daughters in his family and of being those who have been chosen to have access to his very presence and to know him.

Calling involves change

When a doctor, nurse, soldier, police officer or barrister is called, we know that they will give themselves in service to others in particular ways and abide by their profession's ethical code. Their calling impacts on their lifestyle, whether it means they belong to rather elite professional clubs, learn to play golf, condemn themselves to shift work, leave their families behind for months at a time to serve overseas, place themselves in danger in the line of duty, or learn to marshal persuasive arguments at short notice and think on their feet. They may not take to the appropriate lifestyle all at once. People sometimes take time to grow into their professional roles, for good or ill, but changes will occur. This may also be true of our learning to inhabit a Christian lifestyle. But what changes are involved? What movement might we expect for a person who is 'called' in this most fundamental of all senses?

Our calling involves a movement...

- from self to Christ
- from sin to holiness
- from pleasure-seeking to service
- from indifference to love
- from ignorance to truth
- from doubt to trust
- from impurity to purity

- from darkness to light
- from sadness to joy
- from fear to peace
- from alienation from God to friendship with him.[3]

Calling requires a response

Like many, I've often sat at an airport waiting for my flight to be called. You keep an eye on the departure board and an ear cocked for the announcements. Since security measures require us to arrive so early at airports these days, we're normally very grateful when the call eventually comes. If we've been delayed our thankfulness is multiplied. No one in their right mind would hear the call and carry on sitting there without getting up to go to the departure gate. That would be stupid.

So it is with the call of God. We must respond to his initiative if the call is to be of any value to us. We do so through faith and by becoming people who daily follow Christ. Jesus himself warned that 'many are invited, but few are chosen' (Matthew 22:14).[4] The choice of God is only confirmed when one makes a response and accepts the invitation. Calling is not something we fall into; it is something we consciously accept.

What a privilege to be among those who are called. How foolish it would be to ignore the call.

Loved

The second great word Jude uses to describe his readers, and so us, is 'loved', although he expresses it somewhat curiously. They are loved, he says, not *by* God the Father, as we might expect, but rather '*in* God the Father'. Why does he say, somewhat awkwardly to our minds, '*in* God the Father'? Let's hold the question and work slowly towards it as we contemplate the love God has for us.

It speaks of a personal calling

I was born at a fortunate time. A baby boomer, I entered a world that was being transformed and afforded many comforts hitherto unknown. Among the advantages was that I was just too young to be called up for National Service. After World War II all 17- to 21-year-olds in the UK had been required to enlist for two years preparing to fight in war, and then to remain on the reserved list for some years afterwards as well. They were called up to fight for the King.[5] When the time came, an envelope would drop through the letterbox ordering its recipient to report for training. In all, some two million young men were called up. Although the order was issued in the name of the King, the order was an impersonal one. His Majesty did not sit in Buckingham Palace, poring over the names of those he was to conscript, nor did he know any personal details about them. The choice was systematically impersonal. Today, it would be even more impersonal since a computer would select the names, as if they were the winners of a lottery. Even the names today would have been substituted by a set of complicated numbers, devoid of humanity.

Yet when the Lord God, king of the universe, calls people into his service he does so because of love. With deceptive simplicity, John in his first letter twice says, 'God is love' (1 John 4:8, 16). This does not say everything we need to know about God. There is a lot more he has revealed to us about his nature than this. And there is certainly no excuse for reversing the sentence and saying that if God is love then any 'love is God'. In our corrupt human natures our love is always tainted and we may well focus it on evil or selfish objects. Nonetheless, to say that God is love gets very close to defining what is the essence of his character, and to the true nature and heart of God himself.

So, when he calls, he calls because he loves. That call rescues us from all manner of darkness, into lives of significance and relationship, as subsequent chapters will explore, all because he loves us. As he called Peter, James, John, Matthew, Mary, Joanna and others personally to follow him, so he personally, by name, calls us to follow because of love.

It speaks of a gracious calling

The love which accompanies and motivates God's calling on our lives is *agape* love—love of the deepest kind. Grasping the nature of this love, C.S. Lewis wrote, 'Divine Love is Gift-love.'[6] That's exactly in line with John's understanding of agape: 'This is how we know what love is: Jesus Christ laid down his life for us' (1 John 3:16). God's love for us is more than affection, much more than emotion, and certainly nothing like the warm fuzzy feeling we mistake on occasions for falling in love. It is a love that involves active and costly self-giving, seen supremely in the sacrifice of Christ on the cross.

Furthermore, we begin to appreciate the depth of this love when we realise that this is love for the undeserving, for those who have no claim upon it, for those who have no rights over it and who can certainly never repay it adequately. The culture of New Testament times was one that saw relationships in terms of reciprocal exchange. You only invited someone to dinner when it was to your advantage to do so, when having them as your guest would make you look good, or when you could expect a better invitation in return. You did not give to those who could not pay you back. Your love was expended only after careful calculations had been made. How extraordinary, then, is the love of God for us. How totally countercultural.

His call is marinated in grace. We were not called because we were good, qualified, talented, indispensable to God (how absurd to think in those terms) or had the right connections (even more absurd if we think we have more connections than the creator of the universe!). No, it is a calling of grace, of undeserved love. Paul certainly knew this to be true in his own case. He explained to the Galatians, who thought they could earn God's forgiveness by their own efforts, that God set him apart from birth 'and called me by his grace' (Galatians 1:15). He never got over the wonder of his calling, remarking, late in life, to Timothy that given his previous history as a blasphemer and persecutor, his appointment to Christ's service was a sign that 'the grace of our Lord was poured out on me abundantly' (1 Timothy 1:14).

The grace of God extends not just to the initial calling to be a Christian and servant of the living God but to the whole of the Christian life. Jude's readers were under enormous pressure from within the congregation because erroneous and divisive teachers threatened to undermine everything the church had taught up to that point. No doubt the congregation would have been small, so families and friends were all caught up in the controversy. The personal dimensions of it would have been painful, especially for those who wanted to remain true to apostolic teaching. What they needed to know above all else was that they were loved by God. The doctrinal perverts with whom they struggled certainly didn't love them. But it wasn't the love or the opinion of the heretics that counted. God loved them and that outweighed everything else. God's love was sufficient to protect them and keep them going in the fiercest of storms.

It speaks of a planned calling

We are moving towards the question of why Jude says that they were loved 'in God the Father', though we haven't got there yet. 'In' points to something deep and interior. It hints that this love of God is no superficial or hastily thought-up reaction to people's need but a reflection of God's eternal nature and long-established plan. The calling arises from within the heart of God, who, in Paul's words, 'chose us in him before the creation of the world to be holy and blameless in his sight. In love he predestined us for adoption to sonship through Jesus Christ, in accordance with his pleasure and will' (Ephesians 1:4–5). God's love arises from the depths of his being.

It speaks of an intimate calling

It's probably John who sheds most light on what it means to be 'loved in God the Father'. Having said, as mentioned, 'God is love', he immediately adds, 'Whoever lives in love lives in God, and God in them' (1 John 4:16). John writes several times about being, remaining or living 'in' God (1 John 2:24; 3:24; 4:13). John had witnessed the complete oneness Jesus and his Father enjoyed, recalling the way Jesus described it himself:

'Father, just as you are *in* me and I am *in* you' (John 17:21). That, said Jesus, was to be the pattern of his relationship with his disciples. It was to be a triad of intimate relationship: 'I *in* them and you *in* me' (John 17:23, all emphases mine).

Being 'loved *in* God the Father' means 'that those whom God loves are taken into the intimate fellowship of God's love, embraced and enfolded by his love'.[7] It points to the indwelling of the believer in God in a secure, deep and continuous closeness that nothing in life (or the church) can threaten or destroy. God takes the initiative in loving us in Christ as he has loved his only Son.

Kept

Once more Jude's words contain a surprise. We might presume that Jude would have wanted to boost the confidence of his readers by saying that whatever their troubles they were being kept *by* Jesus Christ. It would have been a perfectly legitimate point to make and one that was pastorally apt. However, he does not say they, or we, are kept *by* Jesus Christ but rather 'kept *for* Jesus Christ'.

Kept for the special day

Leading up to Christmas, temptation abounds. The fridge is filled with the most delicious variety of food and the presents are colourfully wrapped under the tree. Plead as one might with one's wife or mother to be allowed to eat the treat or open the parcels a few days before Christmas, the answer is usually a very robust 'No, you can't touch them. They're being kept for Christmas Day.' When Christmas Day arrives, salivating in anticipation gives way to tasting in reality. The presents, whose wrappings may have only hinted at what was inside, will have passed their 'feel-by' date and so are opened to reveal their contents.

In like manner, the Christian is being kept for the day when Christ will come again. Present experience gives only a glimpse of what's to come. New Testament writers often illustrate this in terms of inheritance. Peter, for example, writes of the inheritance which is 'kept in heaven for you' and which as a result can 'never perish spoil or fade' (1 Peter 1:4; see also Ephesians 1:14; Colossians 1:12; 3:24; Hebrews 9:15). Like any earthly legacy, it is being kept safe until the day arrives when the beneficiary can rightfully receive it. On 'the day of Christ Jesus' (Philippians 1:6) Christians will at long last enter into the fullness of their salvation.

But the thought is two-sided, not one-sided. We will enter fully into our inheritance, but Christ himself will also enter into the joy of his work finally being brought to its culmination. New Testament writers thought of this in terms of the arrival of the wedding day when the bride would be revealed in all her glory, to the great joy of the bridegroom. Paul, not without some trepidation (1 Thessalonians 2:17–19), looked forward to the day when 'a radiant church' would be presented to Christ 'without stain or wrinkle or any other blemish, but holy and blameless' (Ephesians 5:27; see also 2 Corinthians 11:2). John equally dreamed of the wedding celebration to come:

Let us rejoice and be glad
and give him glory!
For the wedding of the Lamb has come,
and his bride has made herself ready.
Fine linen, bright and clean,
was given her to wear.
(Fine linen stands for the righteous acts of God's holy people.)
REVELATION 19:7–8

Kept until the special day

In reality, the gap between being kept *for* Jesus Christ and being kept *by* Jesus Christ is not as great as it would seem. The eye does not settle on the distant horizon without passing through the intermediate territory. Keeping the food and presents for Christmas Day necessarily involves making sure they're protected in the meantime. Being kept *for* the day of Christ Jesus necessarily involves being kept *by* Jesus Christ for that day.

Challenges, failures and discouragements are sure to come. But, 'The Lord makes firm the steps of the one who delights in him; though he may stumble, he will not fall, for the Lord upholds him with his hand' (Psalm 37:23–24). Our safe perseverance in the Christian life depends not on our successes, our achievements, or even our progression, but ultimately on his gracious keeping power.

Such a confident assertion of our security does not permit us to be complacent about our Christian life, since it is our 'union with Christ [that] is the ground of our safety and preservation'.[8] Rather, such assurance serves as the greatest of incentives to us to live out our calling more faithfully.

Puritan preachers were great doctors of the soul, always careful to apply the teaching of the truth they expounded. So when Thomas Manton commented on these verses he spoke of the way (to paraphrase) they bring comfort when people are in trouble and God seems to hide his face; when they face temptation and are in hard conflict with doubt and sin; when they face danger and opposition seems tangible; when discouragement comes and the cards seem stacked against them; and when death comes and the final enemy is faced.[9] Kept… kept… kept.

Jude wants to lift his readers' eyes away from their present battles so they can focus on their future destination. It may seem a long way off, just as arriving at a holiday destination does to the child in the car who constantly bugs his parent with the question, 'Are we there yet?' The parent will, of course, truthfully answer no, yet also build hope as confidently as they can, sure that, short of a breakdown, a traffic accident, a tornado or whatever, they will get there. The Christian can be even more confident because of the keeping power of Christ.

If you had to choose three words to describe yourself, which three would you choose? Tall, dark and handsome, perhaps? Loud, fun and untidy? Shy, quiet and studious? Fit, lean and mean? Rich, flamboyant and carefree? How about 'called… loved… and kept'? These are the three most important words concerning our identity in Christ.

Key lesson
Discover your identity in the Christ who calls, loves and keeps you, not in success, position, material possessions or your own passing moods.

Questions
1. If you had to sum up your life in three words, which words would you choose?
2. How conscious are you of the call of God on your life? How important is the call to you?
3. Think about the circumstances when you have especially felt loved and kept by God. Did you express thanks to God at the time? Did you testify to God's grace to others? And how did the experience shape your ordinary day-to-day living in Christ?

2

Called out of darkness

… called… out of darkness into his wonderful light.
1 PETER 2:9

In her Christmas Broadcast in 2015, Her Majesty Queen Elizabeth II commented that the world had experienced 'moments of darkness'. She was referring to the terrorist atrocities in Paris and to other acts of evil that had occurred earlier that year. To most biblical writers, however, to speak only of 'moments of darkness' would have seemed a classic British understatement and far too superficial a description of the human condition. For them, in Isaiah's words, 'darkness covers the earth and thick darkness is over the peoples' (Isaiah 60:2). The tragedy of humanity was not that night fell occasionally but that men and women seemed to live in a perpetual and dense state of gloom, which they were unable to dispel by their own human effort. People live under the power of darkness—in 'the dominion of darkness', to cite Paul (Colossians 1:13)—and need to be rescued from it.

This pessimistic diagnosis of the human situation need not lead to despair but rather to a turning to God, who alone has the ability to rescue people and bring them into the light. Isaiah foresaw the mission of the servant of the Lord as releasing 'from the dungeon those who sit in darkness' (Isaiah 42:7). He spoke of God himself promising, 'I will turn the darkness into light before them' (42:16).

Not for nothing, then, has conversion to Christ often been spoken of as 'seeing the light'. When the Billy Graham Centre was built at Wheaton, Illinois, it was designed as a parable of conversion, with visitors passing through a darkened tunnel before entering into a brilliantly lit room.

The awful anatomy of darkness

Fear of the dark is common. Children are often disturbed by the dark when they try to sleep. Elderly people often fear to go out in the dark for perfectly understandable reasons. They're anxious that they may stumble over an uneven surface or trip over the kerb, or afraid of who might be lurking in the shadows, or that they may get lost and be unable to find their way home. We refer to suffering and other tough times as dark hours. Separation and the death of loved ones are some of the darkest times of all. Darkness stands in contrast to all that is good, healthy, warm, and as it should be.

Was this what Peter had in mind when he said that Christians are 'called out of darkness'?

While it is a common biblical metaphor, two particular New Testament writers dwell on the image in some depth: John and Paul.

John's anatomy of darkness

From the start to the very end of his Gospel, John employs the metaphor of light and darkness in a number of ways, all of which find their resolution in Jesus as 'the light of the world' (John 8:12). He begins by claiming that Isaiah's prophecies have at last been fulfilled: 'The light shines in the darkness, and the darkness has not overcome it' (1:5).[10] Yet he knows that not all share his joy. Rather than welcoming the light, which seems the obvious thing to do, since it is the way to cure the world's ills, the world rejected it and even sought to extinguish it, as it still does. Yet, like one of those candles on a birthday cake that can't be snuffed out and which spring back into life after a moment or two, the light of Jesus was inextinguishable. Numerous attempts were made to silence or remove him, culminating in his trial and execution, but even that could not dispose of him. At the end of his Gospel, John selects his words carefully, recording that it was 'early on the first day of the week, while it was still dark' (20:1) when Mary went to the empty tomb and encountered the Risen Lord. The light had triumphed over the darkness.

Darkness and light vie with each other throughout the Gospel. People faced a fundamental choice: they could live safely in the daylight or they could stumble their way through life as if living in the dark hours of night (11:9–10). The Gospel presupposes that many opt for the darkness. Jesus encountered the darkness in many varied forms. He encountered the darkness of religious prejudice and of obtuse unbelief (8:12–58). He knew that people had lost their way and were floundering around because they believed the devil's lies (8:44). He encountered the darkness of people's suffering, epitomised most of all by the blind man to whom Jesus gave back his sight. Jesus himself explained that his physical disability represented the spiritual blindness of many (chapter 9, especially v. 39). He encountered the darkness of death at the tomb of his friend Lazarus (John 11:11–44). Darkness was on every hand.

Jesus' mission to bring light into the darkness was rejected by many. Since light was surely transparently better than the darkness, why did they do this? John explained the rejection in moral terms, an explanation that still holds true. 'People loved darkness instead of light because their deeds were evil. Everyone who does evil hates the light, and will not come into the light for fear that their deeds will be exposed' (3:19–20). The darkness aids people in clinging on to their shameful behaviour and somehow makes it feel more acceptable. Behaviour they'd never countenance in the light is hidden under the cloak of darkness, which dulls their already defective consciences further and masks their true guilt.

John's musing on the darkness is not purely negative. He wants us to understand the seriousness of our condition in order that we might be encouraged to seek a radical solution. But solution there is. Jesus Christ, 'the light of the world', came to dispel the darkness. But let's explore another critique of the darkness before we ask how he did so.

Paul's anatomy of darkness

John played on the literary dualism of light and darkness to describe the cosmic battle in which 'the light of the world' triumphed. In doing so he gave us a deep, personal and moving account of the gloom from which God delivers people. Paul's anatomy of the darkness is less literary and more analytic.

In a damning critique of the mindset of the Gentiles, which in present-day terms means non-Christians, Paul denounces it as 'futile' and writes,

> They are darkened in their understanding and separated from the life of God because of the ignorance that is in them due to the hardening of their hearts. Having lost all sensitivity, they have given themselves over to sensuality so as to indulge every kind of impurity, and they are full of greed.
> EPHESIANS 4:17-19

Three dimensions, at least, are evident in this critique. First, there is a knowledge dimension: 'they are darkened in their understanding'. They may think themselves 'oh, so clever' but the reality is they are working in the dark 'because of the ignorance that is in them'. It would be foolish to claim that the clever people of Paul's day didn't know a lot. They did. Today, of course, we know so much more than they did, thanks to the advances of science and technology. Our understanding of our universe and how it works (and of much more besides) is staggering in comparison with earlier days. Yet, now as then, human beings have blind spots but are not even aware of them. We can be like people suffering from dementia, awfully confused and forgetful of so much, yet blissfully ignorant of our condition. People's ignorance is an obstacle to their having a true understanding of their human situation, and especially to an understanding of their moral and spiritual predicament.

Many people appear to be real-life versions of Roger Hargreaves'

Mr Clever.[11] Mr Clever knew himself to be 'The Cleverest Person in the World'. But one day he went for a long walk and stepped outside Cleverland and discovered how totally ignorant he really was. In the ordinary world he didn't know any jokes, or any good recipes; he didn't know how to cure the common cold, or what the secret of bravery was, or what people's names were. And as the worm commented when he saw Mr Clever returning to the safety of Cleverland, 'He can't be that clever... he's going the wrong way!' People who know a lot in some areas can be terribly ignorant in others. People who are very intelligent can lack wisdom. Spiritually these are costly mistakes.

Beethoven was so profoundly deaf by the time he composed his Ninth Symphony that he never heard it, except in his imagination. What a tragedy. Likewise men and women are often profoundly deaf towards the God who orchestrated the universe and presides over their lives. He makes no sense to them; he never seriously enters their thinking; and certainly doesn't consciously shape the way they live. If he crosses their mind at all, he does so as a god of convenience to help them out when they are stuck, rather than the Lord God of the universe to whom they bow. This affliction affects all sorts of people, from the most intelligent, like the New Atheists, to the least academically able in our society, who would never gain a single GCSE. Yet, one suspects, it especially strikes the chattering classes and media intelligentsia who often betray a contempt for the poor souls who are religious, and in doing so reveal that they believe they have no need for such superstitions as 'God' and are quite self-sufficient, 'thank you'.

Yet the deafness to God, the blindness, the ignorance, or, to use the biblical image, the darkness in which they are immersed, has profound and negative consequences for the way they live and their enjoyment of God's world.

For, secondly, there is a moral dimension to this dark condition in which 'the Gentiles' live. The way they live is evidence, says Paul, of 'the futility of their thinking' (Ephesians 4:17), that is, its emptiness and vacuity. Paul explores the outworking of this futile thinking in the verses that follow. It leads to desires that are twisted and deceitful (v. 22). Offering the secret of living life to the full, they corrupt life, rob us and 'leave us in the end an empty husk'.[12] The moral compass is not oriented to the true north of God's law but to the self, which determines the direction of everything. So, lying, undisciplined anger, theft, unwholesome talk, bitterness, resentment, sexual immorality, greed and idolatry become commonplace (4:25—5:7).

Of course, not everyone manifests such behaviour all of the time. There are plenty of decent people around. Moreover, the expression of these community-destroying vices can be made to look socially acceptable; they may even be considered virtues by those who do not want to live 'precious' lives or fear being seen as 'good'. Elizabeth Achtemeier once perceptively asked, 'Who wants to be good anymore? We want to be free, self-fulfilled, integrated, successful, admired, even slim and beautiful—but good? No, that is not a sought-after character trait in our time.'[13] We admire a figure like Mother Teresa, but we don't want to be like her. We feel, she continued, that God makes too many demands that 'get in the way of our lifestyles' and 'contradict the easy immorality of our culture'.[14] Her suspicion is justified, for living a godly life does call us to live counterculturally and to reject patterns of living associated with darkness which cost humanity dearly.

This moral deficiency is not only people's misfortune but their fault. John spoke of people loving darkness because their deeds were evil (John 3:19). Paul agrees. The fault line runs deep because people's 'foolish hearts [are] darkened' (Romans 1:21). People collude with the darkness because of 'the hardening of their hearts' and the stubborn resistance to facing sin. They collude with it because it permits them to fulfil their fallen and corrupted natural instincts without blushing. The more they collude with it, the easier it becomes. Consequently, they become insensitive to God and to others and are only motivated by satisfying their own physical instincts.

Thirdly, Paul says there is a spiritual dimension to all this. The worst tragedy of all is that living in darkness means we are 'separated from the life of God'. Darkness brings separation. When we cannot see each other, it is difficult to know each other. What is true naturally is equally true spiritually. God is a stranger to us. Knowledge of him is vague and distant at best, but we cannot say we know him. In truth, we are detached from the source of all true life and disconnected from 'the life-giving power of the one true God'.[15]

Paul has written earlier in his letter about the fatal disadvantages Gentiles suffered because they were separated from Christ (Ephesians 2:1–20).[16] They had none of the advantages that were available to those who were God's chosen people. He had a catalogue of dreadful words to describe the Gentile condition. They were 'disobedient', 'deserving of wrath', 'dead in transgressions', 'uncircumcised', 'excluded', 'foreigners to the covenants', 'without hope and without God', 'far away' (from God), 'strangers'. He sums it all up by saying, 'You were once darkness' (Ephesians 5:8).

We may not fully appreciate all the details or depth of Paul's analysis of Gentile culture and its darkness, but we know our lives are surrounded by darkness. Broken relationships, lies, corruption, empty promises, sickness, destructive addictions, physical and mental abuse, sexual licence, to name but a few of the evils we practise or encounter, and ultimately death, are on every hand.

Paul does not engage in this profound and disturbing critique of Gentile (non-Christian) culture to make people feel guilty or so that he can smugly rejoice in his own righteousness. His purpose is twofold. On the one hand, he seeks to awaken people to their true condition and to give them an accurate diagnosis of their ills. Doctors may be wisely cautious about relaying bad news, but no doctor would be considered ethical, professional or honest if they deliberately withheld a grim diagnosis from their patient because they wanted to be kind to them. The kindest thing to do is to speak the truth. On the other hand, Paul wants the Gentiles to understand the true wonder of God's grace in removing the darkness from their lives and giving them the light of Christ. The deeper the darkness, the greater the light that contrasts with it. The more we confront people with their sinful condition (and no exaggeration is necessary), the greater the grace of God is seen to be.

Perhaps it is because we don't take the depth of darkness in which people live as seriously as we should that we are not motivated to share the light of Christ as much as we should.

The crucial defeat of darkness

Peter's readers were no strangers to unjust suffering and persecution. They must have felt the presence of darkness up close and personal from time to time. But Peter is emphatic. They were 'called out of darkness into [God's] wonderful light'. However dark their environment, they were no longer part of it. Escape from the darkness had been made possible because the darkness had been crucially overcome by the light of Christ.

Paradoxically, that light only dawned when Jesus, 'the light of the world' (John 8:12), himself entered the heart of the darkness. Using parallel illustrations, Tom Smail explains why this should be so:

> Christ comes to the cross as the fireman comes to the fire, as the lifeboat comes to the sinking ship, as the rescue team comes to the wounded man in the Alpine snow. They have what it takes to help and deliver, but they must come to where the fire burns, the storm rages, the avalanche entombs, and make themselves vulnerable to the danger that such a coming involves.[17]

So Jesus needed to enter the darkness. John notes that as his crucifixion drew near, Jesus warned that the light would soon fade and night was approaching (John 9:4–5; 12:35). John highlights that when eventually Judas left the common meal to betray him, 'he went out. And it was night' (13:30). The other Gospels tell us that when Jesus was crucified 'darkness came over the whole land' (Mark 15:33; Matthew 27:45; Luke 23:44). Even though John doesn't mention that happening, the presence of darkness hovers over his account of Jesus' execution. It seemed as if darkness had triumphed. The crucifixion was the darkest moment in history.

However, such a verdict would be premature. It is not over until it is over. After the darkness of Good Friday, and the intervening uncertain day of Jesus' rest in the tomb, the light of Easter Day broke through, conquering the darkness once and for all. Death, the darkest experience of all, had been put in its place. Satan, the father of lies and perpetrator of so much darkness, had been routed. Sin's stranglehold over people had been broken, setting them free to live in the light.

The fact that the light of the world had triumphed is much more than a universally true and incontrovertible historical achievement. As Paul discovered, it was designed to be personally experienced and life transforming. He encountered the light on the road to Damascus and later described his conversion experience as the moment when 'God, who said, "Let light shine out of darkness," made his light shine in our hearts to give us the light of the knowledge of God's glory displayed in the face of Christ' (2 Corinthians 4:6).

In my home town of Torquay there are some prehistoric caves called Kent's Cavern. Any visitor will be told that countless seeds lay deep in those caves, dormant in the darkness for centuries, until workers installed electric light in them. Once the light was introduced the seeds sprang into life. When the light of Christ shines in our lives, life begins. Our minds are illuminated, our wills enlightened and our spirits, which were dead because of sin, are brought to life. The intellectual, moral and spiritual bankruptcy from which the Gentiles suffered is suffused with light, and the transformation of all three dimensions is set in train because of Jesus.

The continuing attraction of darkness

Peter's readers were believers who loved Christ and had become obedient to the truth (1 Peter 1:8, 22), and so he reminds them that they had been 'called out of darkness'. They no longer lived under its power or in its domain but, as Paul would put it, they had been 'rescued... from the dominion of darkness and brought... into the kingdom of the Son he loves' (Colossians 1:13). Darkness no longer described the condition of their hearts, nor the deformity of their wills, nor the emptiness of their minds. They had experienced a 'new birth' (1 Peter 1:3) and were altogether different people. The darkness was left behind. They were new people. This was true, even 'though now for a little while you may have had to suffer grief in all kinds of trials' (1 Peter 1:6).

Perhaps it was those trials that made the old darkness still look attractive to some who were in danger of slipping back to 'the evil desires you had when you lived in ignorance' (1 Peter 1:14). Truth to tell, we do not always want to live as fully in the light as we should. Many years ago, when on holiday on the Isle of Skye, I visited a folk museum. I discovered that electricity had come late to the island and many residents who'd managed all their lives without it were not immediately convinced of its benefits. One crofter was quoted as saying in response to a journalist's enquiry (perhaps tongue in cheek), 'It's wonderful, you know. When dusk falls I can switch on the light. I find it so much easier to light my oil lamp that way. Then I can switch the light off again and enjoy the dim glow of the old lamp.' We're attracted by the familiar and, like the children of Israel in the wilderness who wanted to return to slavery in Egypt when they faced difficulties (Numbers 11:4–5; 14:1–4), we forget how awful living in Egypt, or in the dark, is. Darkness can be seductive, tempting, suggestible, appealing. But remember it is always deceptive, unable to live up to its promise. How foolish it is ever to return to the darkness.

We are called out of it. The darkness belongs to the past. We no longer live there. We are now 'children of the light and children of the day' (1 Thessalonians 5:5). We have been relocated, decisively, to live under the rule of light, in the realm of light. Why should we ever want to return? So we no longer base our thinking on practical atheism and live as if God does not exist. We no longer live according to our society's twisted standards or our self-determined moral standards or purely to satisfy our own desires but according to God's standards and laws. We no longer conduct our lives as if we are strangers to God or, at best, on nodding terms with him, having just the occasional conversation with him, but we are alive in him.

Jesus was not only the light of the world himself but commissioned Paul 'to open [people's] eyes and turn them from darkness to light, and from the power of Satan to God, so that they may receive forgiveness of sins and a place among those who are sanctified by faith in [him]' (Acts 26:17–18). As heirs of the apostolic gospel, our calling still is to turn people from darkness to light, which we can only do if we ourselves have left the darkness behind and live in the light of Christ.

Subsequent chapters explore more fully what it means to live in the light. Here it is enough to rejoice at the decisive change that the light brings and to see the folly of wanting to return to live in darkness.

Key lesson
Leave darkness behind and 'walk in the light, as he is in the light' (1 John 1:7).

Questions
1. What form does darkness take in our world and what form does it take closer to home in your community or more personal life?
2. How far do you see the world in terms of darkness and light; or are you more comfortable with a more tolerant twilight?
3. Why do you think it is that darkness has such a hold on us? Are you aware of its seductive power over your life and, if so, how?
4. The cross of Christ was the darkest moment in history. Why, in your own words, was this so and what difference did it make?

3

Called into fellowship

God is faithful, who has called you into fellowship with his Son, Jesus Christ our Lord.
1 CORINTHIANS 1:9

There is a brand of Christianity which rejoices in being negative. It stresses what we are called *out of* so much that it never quite gets around to saying what we have been called *into*. It's good at condemning the dark and urging people to escape from it, but is less good at introducing people to the light in which they now walk. It is as if it was sufficient for Moses to lead his people out of Egypt only to cut them loose and condemn them to meander aimlessly in the Sinai Desert from then on, to their increasing frustration. The children of Israel stayed in the desert for a generation through their own fault, but God's purpose was always to bring them into the Promised Land.

We have been called '*out of* darkness *into* his wonderful light' (1 Peter 2:9, emphasis mine).[18] That light is refracted through the prism of the New Testament into an array of positive colours. The first we give attention to is our calling 'into fellowship with his Son' (1 Corinthians 1:9).

Some people are very suspicious about 'fellowship'. They may mistake fellowship for the many cups of tasteless coffee, accompanied by stale Rich Tea biscuits, they've been obliged to drink after a church service, as if that's what fellowship is all about. They may be naturally allergic to enforced jollification, cynical about small talk, or merely of an introverted disposition. The poet John Betjeman once spoke for such people when he wrote, 'What makes Grosvenor Chapel perfect for me is that people never bother you there. The whole point of it is that you aren't asked to join something... you aren't being welcomed into a club and made to go to parties and take part in things. You are left alone...'[19]

It is inescapable, however, that a person who is called by God is called into a new set of relationships; first and foremost among them is to have fellowship with his Son, Jesus Christ. A relationship with him is at the heart of the Christian faith.

To be called to enjoy this fellowship is at the same time the simplest and the most profound picture of the Christian life.

Fellowship with whom?

Some years ago a policeman moved in a couple of doors from us when we lived in a tight-knit cul-de-sac. He confessed to me some weeks later that before he'd moved in he had checked us and our neighbours out on the police computer. He wasn't allowed to associate with those who had a criminal record. Obviously, to our relief, we did check out! If you're going to associate with anyone, it's wise to know something about them.

The temptation in understanding this aspect of the Christian's calling is immediately to explore what fellowship means. While this is a good step to take eventually, it's perhaps wiser first to see with whom we are called to have this fellowship. It is enough to know for the moment that, whatever else it means, fellowship is a word that speaks of a relationship. So, who is this relationship with?

The calling is to enjoy the privilege of having fellowship with God's 'Son', who is 'Jesus Christ, our Lord'. The titles trip easily off the tongue because we're so familiar with them, but each makes a momentous claim and carries heavy freight.

- *Son*: although there is a sense in which all people are sons or daughters of God, Paul refers here to his unique Son, the one of whom John said, 'No one has ever seen God, but the one and only

Son, who is himself... in the closest relationship with the Father' (John 1:18) and who made the invisible God visible as he lived among us. His sonship is of a different order from that of the rest of humanity because of his eternal intimacy with God.

- *Jesus*: this is his personal birth name, carefully chosen because it means 'Deliverer' or 'Saviour' and he was destined to rescue 'his people from their sins' (Matthew 1:21). Paul defines this Saviour more fully in the verses that follow. He did not save because he was a great moral teacher, or because he undertook spectacular miracles, or because he confounded people with great philosophy. He saved through embracing folly and weakness and submitting himself to dying on the cross (1 Corinthians 1:18–25). Jesus could not have been Saviour apart from the cross.

- *Christ*: this is not his surname, as we have a tendency to think, but a remarkable title. The Greek world used the word 'Christ' where the Jewish world spoke of 'the Messiah'. The Jewish people expected the Messiah to be the heir to David's throne and they looked for one of royal lineage to come and deliver the nation from its enemies. When King David's great heir and successor did arrive he, Jesus, was somewhat different from what they had expected. He was not a military figure but was, nonetheless, one who delivered all those who believed in him from their true enemies and restored them to their true purpose of serving God. Again, Paul is at pains to emphasise that the only Christ is 'Christ crucified' (1 Corinthians 1:23). His cross was the means by which the enemies were to be defeated.

- *Lord*: in some ways this was the most staggering title of all. While in ordinary use it might mean little more than 'Sir', it is evident that when Christians applied it to Jesus, especially after his resurrection, they meant something much deeper. To the Jews there was only one 'Lord' and that was God. The *Shema* had drilled it into them: 'Hear, O Israel: the Lord our God, the Lord is one. Love the Lord your God with all your heart and with all your soul and with all your strength' (Deuteronomy 6:4–5). In spite of this, to claim that Jesus was Lord, and to live under his authority, quickly established itself as the distinguishing mark of the Christian (1 Corinthians 12:3). To any Roman, there was only one Lord in the world and that was not God but Caesar. Hence, to claim that Jesus was Lord was to claim both that he was none other than God himself, embodied on earth, and that he was the most powerful ruler of the world, before whom Caesar was nothing in comparison. It was spiritually innovative and politically subversive.

This is the one with whom we are called into fellowship.

You may have had the experience of being invited to some special occasion in a celebrity's house, or of being unexpectedly consulted by some important person, or noticed and honoured by someone who is powerful or significant in your eyes, even though you didn't know they knew you. You may have been humbled and overwhelmed by the experience. 'What? Little old me, can you imagine it?' If this has happened, as on very rare occasions it has to me, you tend to live off the story for months! But no such invitation comes anywhere close to the invitation to enter into ongoing fellowship with God's unique Son who is Saviour of the world, King Messiah and Lord over all.

Fellowship means what?

At the very least, fellowship involves companionship, a close sharing with others with whom you have crucial things in common. It is more than casual friendship and much more than being Facebook acquaintances. When Jesus appointed his disciples he chose them to 'be with him' before sending them out (Mark 3:14). Relationship preceded mission. Companionship was prior to service. Unless they had spent time with Jesus, listening to his teaching, observing his lifestyle, watching his interaction with his Father and discovering his passions, they would neither have been able to represent him nor have had anything to offer the needy world to which they were sent.

We know little of Enoch (see Genesis 5:21–24), the father of Methuselah, except that he is an outstanding model of one who had fellowship with God. He is known because he 'walked faithfully with God'. He lived just seven generations after Adam, but by that time the world had already degenerated into violent and destructive wickedness. Yet he chose to be a nonconformist in his culture and make a priority of cultivating companionship with God. He did this in spite of the pressure of becoming a father at the age of 65. Or was it, one wonders, the noisy baby that drove him out of the tent to spend time with God?

Significantly, Enoch cultivated this relationship over a long period of time—300 years are mentioned. The relationship may have oscillated a little over time, as all relationships do, but what was more notable was the long, slow, steady commitment he showed. True fellowship doesn't occur overnight. It takes time to develop. His perseverance paid off because after all that time 'God took him away'. As the young Sunday school pupil somewhat sentimentally explained, 'God and Enoch were out for a long walk one day and hadn't noticed the time going on. When they realised how late it was God said to Enoch, "You're nearer my place than yours, so come home and have tea with me today."' Whatever the actual explanation of Enoch's unusual departure from the earth, he is held up in Hebrews as an example of faith and commended as 'one who pleased God' (Hebrews 11:5–6).

Again, it might be somewhat of a sentimental picture, but the story of Ned Weeks picks up the simplicity of having fellowship with God. In a former age:

> Ned Weeks, a man uneducated and ungifted, but with a heart aflame with love for GOD and for men, did such a remarkable work in the town of Northampton that they gave him a public funeral, when crowds lined the streets with every evidence of real sorrow as the cortege passed. A stranger standing by, on asking who this was, and why all this demonstration, was given, in the rough vernacular, the explanation, 'You see, he was wonderfully thick with the Almighty.'[20]

It was exactly the same with the first apostles. When Peter and John were on trial in the high priest's court for healing a lame beggar, the judges were astonished at their courage since they 'realised that they were unschooled, ordinary men', but what struck them most was 'that these men had been with Jesus' (Acts 4:13). The secret of all they did as ambassadors for Christ was that they had been his close companions for three years in Galilee and Judea, walked the streets and roads with him, talked with him for hours and hours, watched his handling of people, learned his teaching, witnessed his relationship with his Father, and eventually gazed on him from a distance (Luke 23:49) as he died, before repeatedly meeting up with him after his resurrection. They had been participant observers in his mission of bringing the kingdom of God to earth, not uninvolved spectators.

When you spend a lot of time with people you become more and more like them. You pick up mannerisms and ways of saying things that just rub off on you, as, more importantly, do their beliefs, perspectives and values. That's why Proverbs advises, 'Walk with the wise and become wise' and conversely 'associate with fools and get in trouble' (Proverbs 13:20, NLT). To become like Jesus we have to spend time with him. There are no shortcuts to Christlikeness.

This companionship is developed essentially through prayer. It is the oxygen of the soul. That does not mean it easily becomes a part of the rhythm of our spiritual lives just as we instinctively breathe in air. There are plenty of distractions to stop us praying, and difficulties, like the question of apparently unanswered prayer, that put stumbling blocks in our way, and plenty of philosophical questions about prayer to discourage us from practising it. Prayer is a discipline and, like many disciplines and routines, valuable to undertake, even if they are somewhat despised today. As Michael Walker perceptively remarked, 'If we put it [prayer] on one side, for days or for weeks, sometimes for months and years, God will not harass us or nag us, nor even hide himself from us. But we will know… there is a closeness to God that will come by prayer and by no other way.'[21]

Prayer is conversation, and conversation is the way friendship and commitment grow. Friends who have things in common can chat together for hours without difficulty or interruption. Prayer is time to speak with God and be spoken to by him, through Jesus. If we spend most of our time in conversation with other things, with work, sport, leisure, the media, or finances, it is no wonder that those other things become more real than God himself.

This companionship is not, and never can be, one where the partners are equal, as I am sure Enoch well knew. God is very much the senior partner on the journey and he chooses the route and gives the directions. We are wise to walk in his ways. There can be no fellowship with Jesus the Lord apart from obedience.

Amos asked, 'Do two walk together unless they have agreed to do so?' (Amos 3:3). Walking in fellowship with God and his Son is an intentional activity which, like going to the gym to keep fit, requires us to shake off apathy and fight off distractions and stir ourselves into action. But it is the healthiest exercise of all.

Fellowship defined more accurately

All that has just been written is true, yet it falls short of what the Bible means by 'fellowship'. The word means much more than a group of friends hanging out together or enjoying a common interest. It means a deep sharing that involves mutual participation. Anthony Thiselton admits that he might be accused of making heavy weather out of the word but feels compelled to translate it as 'communal participation'.[22] He uses the language of being a shareholder to explain it, where we have a common investment in an enterprise with others. He doesn't say what suggested this metaphor to him but it is interesting to note that when, in Luke 5:10, we read that James and John were Simon's partners in their fishing business, the word used for partners is *koinōnoi*, that is, 'fellowshippers'. They'd sunk (not literally, we hope) their lives and monies into the business and worked hard at it day and night.

Shareholders sometimes do little more than invest some of their money and maybe turn up at the annual general meeting to vote in favour of the chairman's report. But being a shareholder in Christ involves a deep participation in the life we share in him, not just an annual nod of approval in the direction of God as chairman of our world.

What we hold in common, it should be stressed, is neither each other, nor Christian work, nor attending church, but Christ himself. Being a Christian does involve following Christ's example, trying to abide by his teaching and accepting him as our Saviour, but when Paul wants to talk about the essential Christian experience he often resorts to the language of our being 'in Christ', our 'union with Christ', or our participating with Christ. This is fellowship language. The Lord's Supper, Communion, Eucharist—call it what you will—is, Paul says, 'a participation in the blood of Christ' and 'a participation in the body of Christ'. Together, we all share the one cup and the one loaf of Christ (1 Corinthians 10:14–22). That's fellowship.

We have fellowship with Christ as we participate in the experiences that are his. So we join with him...

- in his suffering (Romans 8:17; Colossians 1:24)
- in his death (Romans 6:3, 6–7)
- in his burial (Romans 6:4; Colossians 2:12)
- in his resurrection (Romans 6:4–5, 8–10; Ephesians 2:6; Colossians 2:12)
- in his life (Colossians 2:13; Ephesians 2:5)
- in his glory (Romans 8:17)
- in his reign (1 Corinthians 6:2; 2 Timothy 2:12).

These actual and historic phases of the life of Jesus, the Messiah, are to be imprinted and reproduced in the experience of every believer. Fellowship with Jesus leads to a deep assurance of our acceptance by God and to an intimate relationship with him. This should not be mistaken for a cosy friendship where he soothes away all our headaches and removes us safely from all the tough experiences of life. To have fellowship with him means to participate in his life and therefore simultaneously experience 'the power of his resurrection and participation in his sufferings' (Philippians 3:10). We do not graduate from one to the other. We bear his cross until the day of our deaths and yet equally walk in the newness of his resurrected life.

We are not called to do this alone. Inherent within the meaning of fellowship is the sense that this is corporate. Having fellowship with Jesus can never be about *me* and him. It must always be about *us* and him. That's why Thiselton holds on to the definition of it as 'communal participation'. The church is no optional extra but a major element in God's design of salvation. He's not only rescuing individuals but also creating a new people, who together enjoy fellowship with his Son.

What a privilege to know and be known by Jesus. What a privilege to go beyond superficial acquaintance and enter into deep relationship as we become intimately tied to him. What a privilege to enjoy his companionship, to live his life and, yes, also to carry his cross. Such is the fellowship to which we are called.

Key lesson
The heart of the Christian life is a close companionship and intimate union with Jesus.

Questions
1. Think of close friendships. What makes them work? What effect do they have on the way you think and act?
2. How does your daily routine reflect the priority of cultivating fellowship with Jesus? For example, what time and priority do you give to prayer?
3. In what ways do you reflect the character of Jesus and in what way do you need to become more like him? What steps can you take to reflect him more fully?
4. Can you trace the experience of both the cross and the resurrection in your life?

4

Called to belong

And you also are among those Gentiles who are called to belong to Jesus Christ.
ROMANS 1:6

There used to be a ritual every September in homes up and down the length of Britain. As children went back to school, mums (and it was mums doing this in those days) would spend hours sewing labels into their kids' jumpers, shirts, jackets, caps and the rest of their clothes so that when they changed for PE, their precious children could reclaim their own property. The name tag signified who the clothes belonged to. When we are converted to follow Christ, it is as if he sews his name tag into our lives. We belong to him.

Belonging points to ownership

In Paul's world a vast number of people were owned by others. The lives of slaves were defined by the fact that they belonged to another, until somehow they could perhaps gain their freedom. In Roman law slaves were mere 'chattels' or pieces of property. The Roman politician Varro described them 'as a kind of talking tool'[23] who only differed from other pieces of equipment on the estate in that they could put things into words. Even if they worked for a very considerate master[24] it was still true that their lives were entirely at his disposal. The hours of the day were not theirs to shape, but his. They had no rights and were denied any freedom of choice. The sole purpose of their existence was to do the will of their master, a will they were unable to refuse unless, of course, they were prepared to suffer the dire consequences that would follow if they did. The master also had absolute power over their futures.

Given his social context, it may have been more natural for Paul to speak about a Christian 'belonging' to Jesus Christ than it is in our society where we prize independence and individual freedom so much. Many of his readers would have experienced what it was to be a slave first-hand. Very few may have been masters, but all would have readily understood what he meant. And yet his use of the slavery image is still surprising. Were it not that our nice English translations tend to soften the language, we might have noted that in the opening words of Romans Paul describes himself as 'a slave of Christ Jesus', not 'a servant' as it is so often translated. The Greek word *doulos* was a term of abuse and insult.[25] If we had noted that, we might have stopped in our tracks. Paul, a slave?

First, he was a member of the Jewish race, and ever since being set free from Egypt the Jews had a horror of slavery and did all they could to avoid it. The fear of slavery shaped their national psyche. It might have been true that God had 'brok[en] the bars of your yoke and enabled you to walk with heads held high' (Leviticus 26:13), yet the shame of Egypt still lingered. Consequently, it was deeply ingrained in them that they should never subject others to the sort of treatment they themselves had endured from their Egyptian masters (for example, Deuteronomy 5:15; 15:12–15; 24:17–22). Yet Paul volunteers the fact that he is a slave.

Furthermore, as a Roman citizen Paul had rights and privileges and was not above protecting those rights when the law was likely to ride roughshod over them (Acts 16:35–40; 22:22–29). This makes it even more astonishing that Paul, the apostle, describes himself in such a shameful and degrading way. Yet he does so without hesitation and reservation and sees it as a fitting description not only of himself but of all who are Christians.

Was it not demeaning? Has Christ really come to enslave people? While the fundamental status of the slave was one of shame, as we have described, some slaves could rise in the estimation of their owners and become educated, significant and valued members of their master's household, although they would always carry the stigma of their lack of freedom with them. Besides this, the status of the master had implications for the status of the slave. The higher the status of the master, the more prestige the slave would enjoy. To be a slave to the emperor would have been more honourable than being a slave to some backstreet nonentity. Even today I know several people who have done menial jobs of cleaning and suchlike whose chests have swelled with pride because they were cleaning for a member of the royal family, or even for Lord X, or Admiral Y. As Christians we are called to be slaves of the highest and most noble authority of all. We are owned by and serve Jesus, who is the Christ and, as the previous reflection mentioned, Lord of all. Serving him is an honour which could never be outstripped.

Moreover, Jesus himself serves as the model slave. If he who was the creator of all things and Lord of all could engage in a task reserved for lowly slaves, pick up a towel and wash the feet of his disciples, then what else could his disciples do but becomes slaves? 'No servant,' as Jesus remarked, 'is greater than his master, nor is a messenger greater than the one who sent him' (John 13:16). He had renounced 'equality with God' and the status that involves, and 'made himself nothing, by taking the very nature of a servant [slave]' (Philippians 2:6–7). Could they do less? Furthermore, as Murray Harris has pointed out, having taken on the voluntary role of being a slave of God, Christ transforms our understanding of Christian slavery 'from being a distasteful experience and makes it a privilege and honour'.[26] There was no lack of dignity in him. Rather his service gave him dignity.

People became slaves in all sorts of ways. Some were born into it; for others it was a result of being defeated in war, or of debt, or some other unfortunate circumstances. Whatever got them into this position, however, many would find themselves being sold in the slave market at some stage. They were marketable goods, subject to a sensitive and flexible pricing regime. Paul reminded the Corinthians, 'You are not your own; you were bought at a price' (1 Corinthians 6:19–20). Christians are no cheap option or bargain-basement purchase. Bidding farewell to the church elders in Ephesus, Paul specified exactly what that price was: Christ had paid the ultimate price to purchase them since they were 'bought with his own blood' (Acts 20:28). It was, in fact, common among the apostles to speak in these terms, although each brought their own distinct and complementary contribution to the table. Paradoxically, Peter spoke of 'the precious blood of Christ' (1 Peter 1:19) not as the price paid to enslave someone but as the redemption price paid to set a slave free. John has his eye to the global effect of the purchase when he records the 24 elders singing to the slain lamb, 'and with your blood you purchased for God persons from every tribe and language and people and nation' (Revelation 5:9).

The Methodist Covenant Service, used at the start of each new year, has grasped the meaning of belonging to Jesus Christ well. The Covenant Prayer includes the words:

I am no longer my own, but yours.
Put me to what you will, rank me with whom you will;
Put me to doing, put me to suffering;
Let me be employed for you or laid aside for you,
exalted for you or brought low for you;
Let me be full, let me be empty;
Let me have all things, let me have nothing;
I freely and heartily yield all things to your pleasure and disposal. . .[27]

Belonging points to inclusion

If our freedom-loving culture makes us feel apprehensive at the call to be a slave of Jesus, the second dimension involved in Paul's statement of our calling 'to belong to Jesus Christ' is a reason to marvel.

When I snatch bits of a conversation my wife is having on the phone I'm very likely to get only a partial understanding of what she's saying, if not the wrong end of the stick altogether. Similarly, extracting a few words from a Bible verse can be dangerous. Casting our eyes a little more widely helps us to understand things more fully. Here we see that Paul relates his status as a slave, in verse 1, to his role as a gospel preacher, which, he goes on to explain, in his particular case meant being a preacher of the gospel to the Gentiles, who were also 'called to belong'. In fact, that's essentially his point. He's writing to a Gentile church in Rome and saying to them, 'You also are among the Gentiles called to belong to Jesus Christ.'

The present-day church is almost wholly Gentile. We take this for granted, so much so that we find it difficult to grasp the seismic shift that was required for a Jewish religious community, following a Jewish Messiah, planted in Jewish soil, who saw themselves as bringing to fruition all their Jewish heritage, to step outside their Jewish boundaries and incorporate the Gentiles. Gentiles were unclean idol worshippers and strangers to the living God. They lacked the privilege of having had the law and the prophets. The covenants, the temple, the sabbath, the rite of circumcision and the rules that kept Jews separate meant nothing to the Gentiles. Why, they weren't even monotheists! They believed in any and every god except the one true God. No wonder they had no hope (Ephesians 2:11–22).[28]

Then an extraordinary and unexpected thing happened. Members of the early Christian, but exclusively Jewish, sect began to preach the good news of Jesus to Gentiles. They did it without any forward planning or forethought and caught the apostles on the back foot by their unauthorised activities (Acts 8:1–8; 11:19–24). Peter, the leader of the movement, took some time to reconstruct his thinking, and only then because of the dramatic intervention of an empty stomach, 'a large sheet' and a multitude of 'unclean' animals (Acts 10:1–23). Peter was learning 'that God does not show favouritism' (Acts 10:34) and the gospel of Jesus was for all peoples and nations, and for nasty, dirty and religiously ignorant Gentiles as well as well-brought-up, cleanly scrubbed Jews.

If it took Peter some time to understand that the gospel was for everyone, it took others much longer. The debate runs through the New Testament writings, as the name of a seaside resort runs through a stick of rock. They discussed it in Acts 15 at Jerusalem, but it was still causing problems when Paul returned to Jerusalem in Acts 21. It caused major havoc among the churches of Galatia to whom Paul wrote his fiercest letter about this issue, and even caused fierce disagreement between Paul and Peter, who was still in the process of being reconstructed (Galatians 2:11–21). Paul was still talking about it in his later letters, like Colossians (3:11; see also Galatians 3:28).

And really, that's the main message of Romans. Martin Luther and the reformers personalised it to the great benefit of millions. But in doing so they missed out on seeing that the true focus of Romans is that the gospel is good news for all nations, irrespective of their religious heritage. Gentiles are included as well in the grace of God and can be put right with God because, just as *all* (Jews and Gentiles alike) have sinned, so *all* (Jews and Gentiles alike) can be made alive in Christ Jesus. *All* (Jew and Gentile alike) 'are justified freely by his grace through the redemption that came by Jesus Christ' (Romans 3:24; see also vv. 21–23; 5:12–21). Jewish people do not have access to God and his grace via a superhighway, while Gentiles are condemned to travel a twisty, winding country lane. Both have access through the same route, on the same terms.

So Gentiles who had been 'excluded' (Ephesians 2:12) are now included; outsiders have become insiders. They belong! If you've ever been unexpectedly included in something for which you'd never thought you'd qualify, perhaps by being invited to a party, or joining the membership of a club, you'll know the sense of delight it evokes. You'll also perhaps remember some initial sense of insecurity. 'Does my face fit? Do I really belong here? Will I be found out? Will someone unmask me as a fraud and ask me to leave?' On a rare occasion when I had a legitimate right to enjoy the comfort of a business class lounge at Bangkok Airport, an embarrassing incident occurred when the staff ejected another passenger who didn't have the right to enter and use the facilities. How reassuring then that God in Christ could not make it clearer that anyone who has faith in Christ really does belong, whatever their qualifications or lack of them. It is his qualifications, not ours, that ensure we are included.

Inclusion is high on the current political agenda. Exclusion, based on any form of discrimination, is considered anathema and is increasingly ruled out by legislation. Given that, perhaps a word of caution is in order. Both the senses of belonging which we've looked at so far, and indeed the one we are yet to mention, must be held together. People are not included just because they are Gentiles but because they are Gentiles who have become slaves of Jesus Christ and have faith in him. This has implications for their lifestyle choices and ethical commitments. They aren't included willy-nilly, but included because they have offered themselves as slaves and living sacrifices to God (Romans 12:1). But it matters not one whit whether they were nurtured in a Christian home, were brought up in a Sunday school, have led a reasonably moral life, are an Anglican, Methodist, Baptist, Presbyterian, Pentecostal or whatever, or have none of these credentials. The Gentile who has led an impure life takes their stand on level ground at the cross of Christ alongside the Jew who has observed the law as stringently as possible all their life. But they take up their position on that level ground because they have turned from their old way of life and committed themselves to live under Christ's Lordship from then on.

It stands to reason, too, that when we belong to Christ we also belong to each other. It is impossible to be a solitary disciple since we belong together with other Jews and Gentiles who have accepted the gospel 'regarding his [God's] Son' (Romans 1:2) and received the salvation it offers (1:16). Relationship with fellow believers is as implicit in our call to belong as it is in our call to fellowship, which we explored in the previous chapter.

Inclusion—what a privilege.

Belonging points to obedience

The word of caution we've just given is made explicit in the words that immediately precede Paul's affirmation of Gentiles' belonging. As an apostle to the Gentiles, his commission was to call them 'to the obedience that comes from faith' (Romans 1:5). Belonging involves obedience. 'The first obligation of the slave,' Murray Harris reminds us, 'has always been to serve by obeying.'[29] It is not the slave's place to disagree with their master, to negotiate a different arrangement, or 'to do their own thing'. Their duty is to obey.

Much of Paul's letter goes on to spell out ways in which that obedience will express itself in everyday, down-to-earth living. He takes several chapters (12—15) to do so, covering what the implications are in a wide range of circumstances, such as when we are persecuted, as citizens, and as fellow members of very mixed churches where people will have their own opinions. Almost all aspects of life are there and, for those that are not, principles can be found elsewhere to guide us into the path of obedience (for example, Ephesians 4:17—6:9; Colossians 3:5—4:6). Inclusion involves obedience and obedience involves 'serv[ing] one another… in love' (Galatians 5:13). Like landing lights that need to be lined up properly if the plane is to touch down safely, these three landing lights of ownership, inclusion and obedience need to be lined up if we are to be safely grounded in our belonging to Jesus Christ. To belong is to be owned by Christ as his slave, to be included in his family by his grace, and to be obedient not to our own wills and wishes, but to 'his good, pleasing and perfect will' (Romans 12:2).

Just as my name was sewn into my school jumper all those years ago, let Christ's signature be woven into all your life. You are his.

Key lesson
I am not my own. I am a slave of Christ and because I belong to him I belong also to the community of slaves who have made him their Master.

Questions
1. How do you react to the image of being a slave? What are the implications of it for your Christian life?
2. Christians belong to the greatest international community of all time. To what extent do you positively appreciate that and understand the

privilege of belonging to the church both locally and globally?
3. Review your life and see if there is at least one specific area where you need to stop arguing or debating with your Master and start obeying him.

5

Called to be free

You, my brothers and sisters, were called to be free.
GALATIANS 5:13

The quest for freedom is an enduring human quest. Down through the centuries people have worked for it, lobbied for it, argued for it, fought for it, suffered for it and even laid down their lives for it. When freedom is achieved it is a cause of great celebration, marked by special anniversaries, the building of monuments and the renaming of parks or public squares.

No name is greater in the recent history of freedom than that of Nelson Mandela. On 10 May 1994, in his inaugural address as President of the radically new post-apartheid South Africa, he said,

> Today, all of us do, by our presence here... confer glory and hope to newborn liberty... We have at last achieved our political emancipation. We pledge ourselves to liberate all our people from the continuing bondage of poverty, deprivation, suffering, gender and other discrimination... Never, never, and never again shall it be that this beautiful land will again experience the oppression of one another... Let freedom reign. God bless Africa.[30]

As Christians we are 'called to be free'. The Christian gospel is about a freedom that is more fundamental, more radical and more inwardly transforming than any political, national or social freedom experienced by any people in history. Jesus said, to those who were held captive by the devil's lies and were slaves to sin, that 'the truth will set you free'. By 'the truth' he was undoubtedly referring to his teaching, but it was more than that since he constantly personalised the truth. 'If the Son sets you free, you will be free indeed' (John 8:31–36). He came not only to teach truth but to be himself 'the way and the truth and the life' (John 14:6).

The achievement of Christian freedom

Freedom is often won at a price, as the freedom which Europe has enjoyed since the Second World War reminds us. Our Christian freedom is no exception.

The letter in which Paul speaks about our call to freedom is one in which a particular question that arose among Christian Jews is discussed. Its application, though, is of much wider currency than the specific issue they originally faced. Paul states that they were 'held in custody under the law, locked up until the faith that was to come would be revealed' (Galatians 3:23). One way by which they tried to break out of the prison was to observe that law; in saying this he probably had the major markers of Jewish cultural identity especially in mind, like the food laws, circumcision, and observance of the sabbath. But Paul tells them that if they are thinking like that they are fundamentally on the wrong track. They'll never get their 'get out of jail free' card that way because 'clearly no one who relies on the law is justified before God' (Galatians 3:11). Justified means to be acquitted, to be found in a right relationship with God, and this will never come about by keeping the law.

Why not? For two reasons: first, that's not the way God has arranged things. It was because Abraham 'believed God' that God declared him to be righteous. God's chosen means by which people could be 'justified' had always been to invite them to believe his promise rather than earn his favour.[31] That way anyone, not just those who were good, could experience freedom. It was the same for Abraham as for us. Secondly, trying to achieve freedom by observing the law was bound to fail because, however much people tried, they'd never be able to keep it perfectly, as required, since by nature they were sinful men and women. They'd be forever missing the mark. God's way of justifying people by faith was the only hope people had of gaining their freedom from the condemnation of the law.

Failure to live up to the law's requirement in the first place incurred a penalty and resulted in people being under the curse of God. That sounds incredibly frightening, but Paul has a particular reason for using the word 'curse' rather than judgement or condemnation. God took sin (failure to keep the law or live in agreement with the covenant) very seriously, more seriously than we often do. Of course he does. Sin is not only an insult to him as our creator, but also diminishes us as people made in his image, and is inevitably destructive both of relationships and of his creation. Consequently, God doesn't just open the door of the prison and let people out, regardless. No, he has to be both true to himself and gracious towards his creatures. The word 'curse' gives Paul a way in to explaining how this worked.

Deuteronomy 21:23 laid it down that, following conviction for a capital offence, anyone who was executed was to have their body displayed on a pole and that such people were 'under God's curse'. Now it doesn't take much imagination to think in terms of crucifixion on a cross as being 'hung on a pole'. So, says Paul, when Christ was crucified he was under the curse. But this was clearly not a just verdict as far as his own life was concerned, since he was the one person who had kept all the law and embodied the covenant perfectly.[32] No, says Paul, he was not under the curse for his own disobedience and failure but for ours. In this way, 'Christ redeemed us [that is, bought our freedom] from the curse of the law by becoming a curse for us' (Galatians 3:13). The redemption price was high—none other than the life of Christ himself—but it secured the freedom of all those who were accused and justly condemned for their failure to live up to the law's demands.

The threats to Christian freedom

Religious people seem attracted to rules as much as little children are attracted to puddles and mice are attracted to cheese. Like long-term prisoners who have become institutionalised, many Christians seem incapable of enjoying their freedom for long before they desire to return to the security of submitting to rules. There may be good reasons for this, not least of which is a longing to please God and not to abuse their freedom. They think that one way to ensure this is to live by a new set of rules, whether they be self-imposed or imposed by the community to which they belong. Guidelines which lead us to live disciplined lives are good but are too easily perverted and become precisely the sort of burden from which Christ came to set us free. From the Pharisees onwards this is an understandable but fatal mistake. Seeking to please God by living under rules and regulations is counterproductive and disrespectful, to say the least (Paul uses stronger language), to the Christ who died to set us free.

Galatians and Colossians both provide illustrations of the 'gate fever' which Christians find hard to let go.

Among Galatian Christians

Galatian Christians had been unsettled by itinerant preachers who tried to persuade them that faith in Christ was a good starting point for the Christian life but not sufficient to sustain it. If they were to be genuine Christians, they had been told, faith was a great first step, but to become mature Christians they needed to go beyond it and adopt a whole raft of Jewish cultural regulations and norms which Paul called 'works of the law' (Galatians 3:10). Their point seemed to be justified since, when he visited Antioch, Peter, the senior apostle, observed the Jewish food laws which forbade Jews from eating with Gentiles and, in bad faith, he excused himself from sitting at the table with them (2:11–21). The food laws were one particular example of Jewish laws, but circumcision was another. The itinerant preachers wanted to impose these regulations on Gentiles as well as Jews. In this way, the freedom Christ came to give receded into the background faster than any stationary car you've overtaken in your rear-view mirror.

Paul would have none of it and denounced such teaching in the most forceful of terms. Jews could carry on observing these rules if they liked, but they made no difference to one's standing before God, either for Jews or Gentiles, which was solely and exclusively dependent on faith in Christ. To pretend otherwise was to '[desert] the one who called you to live in the grace' of God. It was to preach a different gospel and to place oneself under God's curse. It was to pander to human arguments and traditions (Galatians 1:6–12). To believe this was to fall under a spell and to betray the Christ who was crucified for them (3:1). It was to render pointless everything they had experienced of God's grace up to this point (3:4). To impose such rules was not a matter of a difference of opinion but a fundamental error, since it undermined the gospel of Jesus Christ completely.

Among Colossian Christians

Paul had never met the Colossian Christians and his tone when addressing them is a little gentler, but the urgency of correcting the similar, but not identical, error they faced is still evident. The Colossians were not quite sure that Jesus and his death were sufficient to truly set them free from their enemies, so they hedged their bets by believing in Jesus but supplementing him with all sorts of other religious practices and regulations. They were in danger of being taken 'captive' (Colossians 2:8) by seemingly beneficial and deceptively religious traditions. Their would-be jailers needed to be unmasked and exposed for the frauds they were.

The threats came from all directions, according to Colossians 2:8–23. There were the human philosophies and traditions that offered a radically different solution to their problems from that of the gospel. There was the religious rite of circumcision that was supposed somehow to enable them to deal with their sinful natures. There was the worship of angels that gave them access to high-octane religious experiences denied to ordinary people. Above all there was just the constant pressure to live by a certain dietary regime, to observe a religious calendar, and submit to ascetic treatment that was designed to subdue the body and repress the temptations within. None of these had any value, Paul claimed, since the whole problem had been dealt with by the cross of Christ. There, he had 'disarmed the powers and authorities' and held them up to public ridicule, exposing them for the failures and swindlers they were (2:15).

Christ had set people free from the prison 'of darkness' and brought them into the kingdom of God's Son (Colossians 1:13). He brought peace into being 'through his blood, shed on the cross' (1:20). To believe otherwise was to place oneself in jail all over again.

Among contemporary Christians

Christians perpetually fall into the trap of substituting rules for faith. Each age and denomination has its own set of rules and regulations, of course. For some it's fish on Fridays, confession on Saturdays and keeping holy days of obligation. For others it's how often you attend church, or whether you have a daily devotional practice which you never fail to keep. Yet others think what's important is how you dress, which version of the Bible you read, or what language you use, with some majoring on how you address God in prayer. More recently, for some what counts is adopting a particular stance on pacifism, environmental issues, where you buy your bananas from, or a number of other contemporary political topics. For others it is about particular practices regarding money, or what TV programmes you watch.

Many of these things may be beneficial in themselves, but they so easily become distorted and supplant the good news that we are put right with God not by any works of the law, however great or however small, however traditional or however recent. We need to be constantly on our guard against these threats to our freedom in Christ.

The nature of Christian freedom

Good Christian people often get very worried at this point. How can this be? Doesn't such a radical gospel just give rise to anarchy? Haven't we learned anything from history? Virtually no nation that in recent years has overthrown a strong government which used to impose the iron rule of law has benefited from the freedom that has been won, but has simply opened the door to competing forces and factions and degenerated into lawlessness. The end result has often been worse, at least for some time, than the oppression it sought to overthrow. Isn't it the same with us and freedom in Christ? Doesn't Paul's gospel mean Christians can go on living how they like, including carrying on sinning?

These questions are not new and were thrown at Paul in his own day. He addresses them in his longer letter to the Romans, in chapter 6, and also in Galatians 3:13—6:6. He sets out how freedom in Christ shouldn't lead to sinful disorder but rather to our becoming like Christ. There is, he insists, no need to curtail the freedom we have in Christ. Let's examine his explanation through that passage in Galatians.

First, think negatively

Freedom is not licence to live how you want. No one thinks the freedom of the road means they can drive in the middle of the road at whatever speed they like, regardless of others. There's no freedom in that. It's likely to end in tragedy, as some of the funerals I have attended and even conducted testify. We don't even need speed limits or white lines to tell us not to drive like that. It's wise not to do so, regardless of the rules. Laws may restrict liberty but often they enhance it, especially when based on wisdom.

So, Paul states, you don't use this freedom in Christ 'to indulge the flesh' by living immoral, impure or debauched lives. Misusing sex, taking drugs, imbibing too much alcohol and eating too much of the wrong things is a false freedom that will eventually rob us of life rather than improve it. Nor do we use this freedom to engage in religious rituals of any sort that we may fancy. Worshipping idols and practising witchcraft, or a host of other non-Christian religious practices, however fashionable, are equally detrimental to the cause of freedom and impose new burdens on people rather than leading them to freedom.

Secondly, think positively

Where do we find freedom? We find freedom in serving 'one another humbly in love' (Galatians 5:13), just as Christ did. Freedom does not lie in serving one's own interests and ambitions first but in serving others first. That means not just thinking nice things about others but actually doing something for them, or else it's not service. That sounds odd. Surely we find greater freedom when we put ourselves and our own interests first? But we don't, simply because that isn't how God wired us up. He made us to find maximum enrichment by serving others rather than ourselves. All the recent studies in happiness confirm the truth of this. Lord Layard, then of the London School of Economics, summed up extensive research into happiness like this: 'Enough to say here that people who care about other people are on average happier than those who are more preoccupied with themselves. More anxiety comes from striving to "do well" for yourself than from striving to "do good" for the rest of the world.'[33]

This shouldn't surprise us since we are made in the image of God, who shows himself to be both a sociable God—'Let *us* make mankind'—and a generous God who reaches out to create a world rather than remaining locked up in himself.

We cannot enjoy freedom in Christ unless we are committed to and serving others. Paul illustrates in this passage what it means to serve others. It means keeping in step with them and neither going too fast in our superiority nor dragging our heels in inferiority (5:25–26). It means humbly restoring those who trip up and sin (6:1). It means relieving those who are overburdened, like the few who take on too much in church or those who are at a stage of family life when they can't quite cope (6:2). It means playing one's own part responsibly without any sense of competition towards others. Behind much of what Paul writes in these verses is the image of the army, and at this point he is saying, 'Carry your own kit bag.' If you don't, it will be someone else who'll have to do it for you and the army will be weaker.

Nelson Mandela put his finger on this in his inaugural speech, from which I quoted at the beginning of the chapter. He said, 'We have not taken the final step of our journey, but the first step on a longer and even more difficult road. For to be free is not merely to cast off one's chains, but to live in a way that respects and enhances the freedom of others. The true test of our devotion is just beginning.'[34] Paul would have said 'Amen' to that.

Thirdly, think spiritually

Paul's mind increasingly turns to the role of the Holy Spirit. Avoiding 'the acts of the flesh' and serving one another in love is not a matter of rules but of God's life within us being expressed.

He uses the organic image of fruit-bearing (Galatians 5:22–23). An apple tree produces apples because it has the DNA of an apple tree. Its fruit is an outworking of the life principle within it. An apple tree doesn't produce cod and chips, or computers (no advertising intended!), but apples. And if we belong to Christ, his Spirit is living within us, so the fruit we will produce is Christlikeness. And what will that look like? Paul does not leave this as a vague principle but spells it out so that it's something we can all understand. To produce the fruit of the Spirit is to live a life of 'love, joy, peace, forbearance, kindness, goodness, faithfulness, gentleness and self-control'. Oh dear. Many would rather believe that it meant singing another worship song and being lost in wonder, love and praise. These qualities are rather more practical and down-to-earth than that.

After talking about the fruit of the Spirit Paul introduces the military image. He says we are to march 'in step with the Spirit' (Galatians 5:25). There is no freedom in setting our own pace, determining which foot we want to put first or which route to take. We'd just trip over one another and pull against one another. We do everything under the command of the spiritual regimental sergeant major (that may not be the best analogy, but you know what I mean). It is only as the army functions together under one command that its soldiers can be effective and free.

Freedom, you see, isn't found in obeying rules, as many Christians think, but by expressing the life of Christ from within and walking in harmony with the life-giving and sovereign Holy Spirit. Perhaps there is no better illustration of this than the parable that we wrongly call the parable of the prodigal son. As Jesus tells it, it is the parable of a man who had two sons, and Jesus leaves us with the puzzling question as to which one of them really was the prodigal (Luke 15:11–32). Remember, the story is aimed at 'the Pharisees and the teachers of the law' who were muttering against Jesus, precisely because he hung loose to their precious rules (15:2). The better known younger son is a wastrel who lives a life that would bring shame on his family, quickly gets through his inheritance, and then in desperation returns home expecting very little but asking to be taken back and given a humiliating and lowly paid job. The older son would never have had the courage to leave home. He was heavy on loyalty, duty and earning his living. He didn't enjoy any freedom in serving his father. His pent-up frustration poured out when, rounding on his father for profligately celebrating the return of his younger brother with a party, he protested: 'All these years I've been slaving for you and never disobeyed your orders. Yet you never gave me even a young goat so I could celebrate with my friends' (v. 29), forgetting to add, of course, that he wouldn't have known how to party if he'd been given the opportunity! He denied himself the freedom he should have enjoyed in his relationship with his father.

When serving becomes duty, worship becomes obligation, and right living becomes law, we're just like the older brother and have forgotten that we are called to be free. Paul insists, 'It is for freedom that Christ has set us free. Stand firm, then, and do not let yourselves be burdened again by a yoke of slavery' (Galatians 5:1).

Key lesson
We need to learn to live wisely in freedom and not be cowed by religious rules and regulations.

Questions

1. Why is it that so many Christians seem anxious and burdened in their serving God, rather than being free?
2. How do you assess your own relationship with God on the freedom scale?
3. Can you identify actual or potential rules, traditions and practices that rob you of your freedom in Christ?
4. Discuss what true freedom looks like. Can you identify some practical steps that may help you to make progress in freedom?

6

Called to holiness

He has saved us and called us to a holy life.
2 TIMOTHY 1:9

Just as he who called you is holy, so be holy in all you do; for it is written: 'Be holy, because I am holy.'
1 PETER 1:15

Freedom in Christ releases us to be what he intended us to be. It permits us to restore God's marred image in us and reflect his character in a fallen and needy world. While the indescribable God is described in many ways, one of the earliest ways he described himself was to say, 'I am holy' (Leviticus 11:44, 45; 19:2). There are some cheeses which once you get them past your nose turn out to be delicious. Holiness is like that. It carries with it the whiff of medieval monasticism, of unjoyful and unlovely Puritanism, or of Victorian legalism. But if you can get past the aroma (in this case, the false aroma) to the word itself, you find a wonderful, multidimensional word, full of meaning.

At its core, holiness is about being set apart, being different. As God reveals himself, so we discover that God's holiness points sometimes to his utter transcendence, at other times to his sovereign power, at others to his moral purity and at still others to his absolute perfection. John Hartley put it rather well: 'Holiness is the quintessential quality of Yahweh. In the entire universe, he alone is intrinsically holy... that means he is exalted, awesome in power, glorious in appearance, pure in character.'[35]

Astonishingly, the first time God commands his people to 'be holy, because I am holy' he does so in the midst of those obscure food laws you read (or, probably more accurately, don't read) in Leviticus. You would have expected such a command to have been proclaimed in the temple with trumpets blaring and multitudes of angels as a backing group. But as it is, it's said in a discussion about the menu! That raises lots of questions,[36] but for our purposes the important thing to grasp is just this: holiness has to do with the whole of life, not just the religious bit of it. Holiness impacts on the way we behave in the kitchen, the lounge, the bedroom, the playroom, the schoolroom, the boardroom, the factory floor, the holiday hotel; in fact, wherever.

Why is holiness important?

Holiness is so important that when Paul wrote to his recent converts in Thessalonica he rather laboured the point and spelled out seven reasons why we should work at it with all our might, in 1 Thessalonians 4:1–12.[37] It wasn't that they were not trying and were useless at it. Rather he was giving them a number of incentives to please God by their living 'more and more'. Here are the reasons for holiness:

1. Because God wills it (v. 3)

When we speak about God's plan for our lives the one thing we can be sure about is that he wants us to be holy. His plan is not that we should be rich, famous, successful, married, secure or even comfortable, but that we should be holy. The command of Leviticus is by no means confined to the Old Testament. It is for us Christians as well, which is why Peter repeats it in 1 Peter 1:15. The popular TV programme *Room 101* is built around the idea that there are things you are best off without in life, so you consign them to Room 101, never to be seen again. But Hebrews 12:14 tells us that one thing we cannot do without if we want to see the Lord is holiness. It must never be consigned to the Christian version of Room 101. Holiness matters because it matters to God.

2. Because Jesus commands it (v. 2)

Paul explains that his instructions about holiness are not something that have come from his own creative imagination, still less from a party of consultants advising the apostles as to how they can make the church more attractive. They are 'instructions we gave you by the authority of the Lord Jesus'. That makes sense since, as Paul says elsewhere, he 'gave himself for us to redeem us from all wickedness and to purify for himself a people that are his very own' (Titus 2:14).

3. Because love requires it (vv. 4–6, 9–12)

Put simply, holiness is the most socially constructive way to live. It benefits others. Sinful living depletes social capital and destroys families and community. Holy living invests in families and builds strong and healthy communities. Paul says as much when he calls people to be holy in the sexual realm and says that we need to control our sexual appetites so that 'in this matter no one should wrong or take advantage of a brother or sister' (v. 6).

Incidentally, while Paul illustrates this in terms of sexual behaviour here, holiness isn't just about sex, by any means. Having talked about sexual purity to begin with, he goes on to talk about social responsibility immediately afterwards. Both have implications for holiness.

4. Because judgement encourages it (v. 6)

While he doesn't make too much of it, Paul rightly lays all his cards on the table and talks about judgement. Living an unholy life, which involves disobeying God's laws and disrespecting others, will result in judgement. We are accountable beings who will one day 'appear before the judgment seat of Christ' to 'receive what is due to us for the things done while in the body, whether good or bad' (2 Corinthians 5:10).

5. Because conversion necessitates it (vv. 7–8)

Conversion to Christ is never a matter of securing your ticket to heaven for the future, but is about starting a life journey of transformation in the present. It is true that when God called us he pardoned us, forgave all our sins, and assured us of eternal life. But implicit within that call is also a call for us 'to live a holy life'. One of the ways we can distinguish between true and fake conversions is whether we can see a commitment to change.

6. Because the Holy Spirit enables it (v. 8)

All this might be a burdensome lesson in self-improvement, except that Paul's next phrase puts all these instructions in a totally different light. We are called to obey God in pursuing a holy life, 'the very God,' he adds, 'who gives you his Holy Spirit'. The Holy Spirit is the resident member of the Trinity who lives within us and brings the life-transforming power of God to bear on our tiny lives. Progress in holiness does not result from our moral effort, although our commitment and determination are required, so much as from God changing us from within and producing the fruit mentioned in the last chapter. The Spirit who 'hovered over the waters' at the beginning and was instrumental in bringing creation into existence is the same Spirit who is in the process of re-creating us. He goes under many names, but most commonly he is called 'the Holy Spirit'. The danger with that is that we take the word 'Holy' for granted rather than realising it means that he is the unique, divine Spirit who is sent by the Holy God on a mission to make us holy.

7. Because witness requires it (v. 12)

Paul ends his list of incentives to holiness where we often start. But he charts the better map by doing so. We're usually very pragmatic. The most frequent accusation hurled at Christians, whether legitimate or not, is that they are hypocrites. We know that living sinful lives will not encourage people to believe our gospel, so we try, however inadequately, to 'win the respect' of those outside the church. It's true:

if we are to gain respect and win others to Christ we must adopt a clean lifestyle. Otherwise our gospel will be dragged in the mud. Hopefully we'll live holy lives for better reasons than wanting to grow the church. Hopefully we'll live holy lives because it is right to do so and because it matters so much to God. But, as a footnote, it will do no harm in commending the gospel to others.

What does holiness mean?

An old TV advert for BT (British Telecom) had Maureen Lipman visiting the sales, only to discover that every bargain she went to buy was already sold and had someone's name stuck to it. The point, of course, was that if only she'd rung BT she could have reserved the machine for herself and made sure she got the bargain she wanted. In a funny way, that's not a bad description of holiness. Holiness means we've been set apart. The 'Sold' notice is on us and we've been reserved exclusively to live as God wants us to. We're not available to live as others might dictate—whether other people, social institutions, cultural fashions, or other so-called deities. Our task is to imitate the moral character of God in our world.

For the children of Israel it all began with the choice God made. 'The Lord... has chosen you,' they were told, 'out of all the peoples on the face of the earth to be his people, his treasured possession' (Deuteronomy 7:6). The choice was not made on the basis of any qualities that were inherent in Israel itself, but was made purely on the basis of God's grace (7:7–8). The choice was publicly launched, as it were, when Moses, observed by the people at a distance, encountered this awesome God on Mount Sinai. There God issued the invitation: 'Now if you obey me fully and keep my covenant, then out of all nations you will be my treasured possession. Although the whole earth is mine, you will be for me a kingdom of priests and a holy nation' (Exodus 19:5–6).

What it meant to keep the covenant took some spelling out. But it all boiled down to that simple rule, 'Be holy, because I am holy.' In other words, reflect my character in the world. Be like me so that people will get a glimpse through you of my otherwise invisible being.

All this went up a gear with the coming of Christ, but it was really the same message, as the New Testament writings emphasise.

What does holiness look like?

That's all very well. But can we be less abstract and more concrete? Yes we can. Holiness has at least six dimensions.

1. Fear of God

I almost softened the words 'fear of' and used the more familiar 'reverence for' instead. But it's all too easy to lessen the element of creaturely awe that we humans should sense before our Maker if we go for the more common word. Fear does not mean we are required to exhibit a cringing terror before Almighty God, but it does mean we know our tiny place before this awesome God and 'tremble at his word' (Isaiah 66:5). It leads us to carefully and consciously obey his commands and restrains us from doing wrong (Nehemiah 5:15). As Ecclesiastes wisely says, remember that 'God is in heaven and you are on earth, so let your words be few' (Ecclesiastes 5:2).

2. Likeness to Christ

One of the all-time classics on holiness was written by J.C. Ryle, the first Bishop of Liverpool, in 1877. In it he wrote,

A holy man [sic] will strive to be like our Lord Jesus Christ. He will not only live the life of faith in Him and draw from Him all his daily peace and strength but he will also labour to have the mind that was in Him, and to be 'conformed to His image' (Romans 8.29.) It will be his aim to bear with and forgive others, even as Christ forgave us—to be unselfish, even as Christ pleased not Himself—to walk in love, even as Christ loved us—to be lowly-minded and humble, even as Christ made Himself of no reputation and humbled Himself. He will remember that Christ was a faithful witness for the truth—that He came to do His Father's will—that He would continually deny Himself in order to minister to others—that He was meek and patient under undeserved insults...[38]

And so he continues, drawing attention to Jesus' compassion for sinners, uncompromising attitude to sin, indifference to human praise, going about doing good, consistency in prayer, and refusal to let anyone or anything stand in the way of his doing God's will.

That's certainly enough to be going on with!

3. Avoidance of sin

We are to have no truck with sin and give it no quarter in our lives. It's not a matter of seeing how close we can sail to the wind before we provoke God to discipline us; rather it is a question of how we can be the best that we can be for God. So we recognise the horror of all sin and avoid it, even seemingly small sins. Jeremy Taylor, the Anglican divine and supporter of the Stuarts, once wrote, 'No sin is small. No grain of sand is small in the mechanism of a watch.'[39] Today we might talk of sharing a bed with a mosquito. Little things can bite, fatally.

Avoiding sin may well mean we submit ourselves to a range of disciplines or limitations so we don't put ourselves in the way of temptation. There may be certain magazines, films and TV programmes, websites and social media connections, which are unhelpful. Equally there may be certain people or places to avoid, as Psalm 1 suggests.

4. Purity of heart

Holiness has as much to do with our inner attitudes as our outward actions. Purity of heart points to our single-minded devotion to please God, through and through. It covers attitudes and character: what we are, not just what we do. So it causes us to check our motives, to become alert to our weaknesses and vulnerabilities, and to be self-aware. Holiness cannot co-exist with hypocrisy. It calls for us to discard the mask of spiritual professionalism that parades our own righteousness while covering up evil within. It calls for integrity.

5. Love in relationships

Mark Twain's well-known quip that he was 'good in the worst sense of the word' aptly describes some Christians. They think that holiness lies in the avoidance of doing wrong and they steer clear of the rocks by a million miles. But there is little that is warm or attractive about them. They've no experience of the freedom Christ came to give, as explored in the previous chapter, and they show no evidence of the love which so characterised him. Their holiness is cold, clinical and calculating. But true love is quite the opposite. Jesus, who is the only perfectly holy person who ever lived, was warm and approachable. Others sought his company, except for the Pharisees, of course. He exuded love. Love and holiness belong together since holiness is about *loving* God with all our hearts and *loving* our neighbours as ourselves.

6. Right living in society

What we have said so far might run the danger of producing pious individuals who are busy about church business but rarely break out of the confines of their religious subculture. While holiness calls us to be set apart for God, it calls us neither to sever relationship with others nor to escape from the world into a sacred ghetto (1 Corinthians 5:9–10). A biblical vision of holiness leads us to be involved in the broken world, just as Christ was, administering healing, shedding love and standing for justice. Unless we adopt the prophetic vision of holiness seen in Micah 6 and Isaiah 58, our understanding of holiness is deficient.

How can holiness be achieved?

The pursuit of holiness is the journey of a lifetime. There are no shortcuts to our goal, no quick solutions, no secret formula, no three easy steps. We struggle and strive, walking in a zigzag rather than a straight line. When we fail we pick ourselves up and by the grace of God carry on. We never graduate from this calling, until our journey is over.

Yet we may be helped on that journey by...

- taking sin seriously;
- going to Christ frequently;
- surrendering life daily.

Perhaps we're back to where we were. Our calling is to have fellowship with Jesus, and if there is a secret to holiness it is in staying close to him. 'If you remain in me and I in you, you will bear much fruit; apart from me you can do nothing' (John 15:5).

Key lesson
God's plan and priority for my life is that I should be holy.

Questions
1. When you hear the word 'holy', what images does it conjure up in your mind?
2. List ten priorities you have for your life. Be honest and be practical. Does holiness figure on the list? If so, where does it come? If not, why doesn't it matter to you?
3. Think further about steps you can take to make progress in holiness.

7

Called to peace

God has called us to live in peace.
1 CORINTHIANS 7:15

Let the peace of Christ rule in your hearts, since as members of one body you were called to peace.
COLOSSIANS 3:15

There are some days when I envy those who are cast away on Radio 4's *Desert Island Discs*. How wonderful to be put ashore on a sun-drenched island with nothing to disturb us except the gentle lapping of the sea and the rich sounds of the music we have chosen (whose volume is under our own control) while we read the books and enjoy the luxury we took with us. No ringing phones, no bickering kids, no noisy traffic, no ghastly muzak, no jabbering media, no intrusive emails and no nagging boss. Peace.

Peace: a great biblical theme

The wonderful words with which Aaron blessed the people of Israel reached their conclusion in the line, 'the Lord… give you peace'. That one word 'peace' enveloped all the other particular elements that Aaron had mentioned, those of God's blessing them, keeping them and shining on them (see Numbers 6:24–26).

Even before the peace of Eden had been destroyed, God's desire had been to see that peace restored (Ephesians 1:4). Throughout the tortuous history of Israel there were periods when the people entered into the peace God longed to give them. Gideon built an altar and called it 'The Lord Is Peace' (Judges 6:24). David could rejoice that 'the

Lord blesses his people with peace' (Psalm 29:11). Yet for the most part peace was elusive.

The prophets, often patiently and creatively, explained to the people why they did not experience more of God's peace. There was, they taught, a connection between peace and righteousness. Peace was 'the fruit of righteousness'. Quietness of spirit was the result of righteous living (Isaiah 32:16–17). 'Righteousness and peace' go hand in hand, or, in the more poetic image of the Psalms, 'kiss each other' (Psalm 85:10). They are necessary allies and companions. To 'seek peace and pursue it' requires that we 'turn from evil and do good' (Psalm 34:14). The experience of peace flowing 'like a river' and 'well-being like the waves of the sea'—constantly refreshing, always sufficient and alive— is only available for those who pay attention to God's commands (Isaiah 48:18). That's why the well-known text, which is often quoted by harassed and overtired workers in jest, is altogether more serious than its common use suggests: '"There is no peace," says my God, "for the wicked"' (Isaiah 57:21). Peace and sinful living are as incompatible as a fox in a hen house, which means that peace and injustice, peace and prideful arrogance, peace and hating one's enemy, peace and stirring up trouble, peace and gossip, peace and any other way in which we refuse to walk in the ways of the Lord are a total mismatch.

When Israel did walk in the ways of the Lord it did not always insulate them from trouble or conflict. Being at the crossroads of the ancient world, their country proved a happy marching ground for armies. Being small made them vulnerable, and victims of the ambitions of their more powerful neighbours. Regardless of their outward circumstances, however, they could know the deep peace of God within, providing they placed their trust in him and did not hitch their hopes to false gods. Jeremiah thundered against the way in which false prophets spoke of political expediency as the way to peace (Jeremiah 6:14; 23:33–40), and pointed out that they were delusional to think that because they had the temple, the symbol of God's presence among them, they would automatically be safe, regardless of whether they obeyed his laws or not (7:1–29). They would, he said, never find peace by dressing their wound superficially when drastic surgery was required (6:14; 8:11). Only by repentance, by the rejection of false prophets, and by trusting in the living God would peace return.

The biblical word for peace—*shalom* in Hebrew—is a big word, meaning far more than the lack of conflict, disturbance or noise. It is a positive word that points to all-round well-being. Writing about the ethics of war, Bishop David Atkinson grasped its meaning well when he wrote,

> … *shalom* covers much more than merely the absence of war. Shalom is rather the absence of disorder at all levels of life and relationship. Shalom includes everything God gives for human beings in all areas of life. It means well-being in the widest sense of the word…

> Peace, then, is about being in right relationship, but it is more even than that. 'Peace' at its highest is about the *enjoyment* and *satisfaction* of being in right relationship—with God, with neighbour, with oneself, with one's environment.[40]

The biblical vision of peace has never been expressed more wonderfully than in the vivid and family-friendly imagery that Micah employed when the nations implored:

> *'Come, let us go up to the mountain of the Lord,*
> *to the temple of the God of Jacob.*
> *He will teach us his ways,*
> *so that we may walk in his paths.'*
> *The law will go out from Zion,*
> *the word of the Lord from Jerusalem.*
> *He will judge between many peoples*
> *and will settle disputes for strong nations far and wide.*
> *They will beat their swords into ploughshares*
> *and their spears into pruning hooks*
> *Nation will not take up sword against nation,*
> *nor will they train for war any more.*

> *Everyone will sit under their own vine*
> *and under their own fig-tree,*
> *and no one will make them afraid,*
> *for the Lord Almighty has spoken.*
> *All the nations may walk*
> *in the name of their gods,*
> *but we will walk in the name of the Lord*
> *our God for ever and ever.*
> MICAH 4:2–5

Nations generally, and the United Nations in particular, which has Isaiah's version of these words (Isaiah 2:4) carved on a wall outside its HQ, love the middle bit about swords into ploughshares and spears into pruning hooks, but they prise them from the words that come before and after, failing to see that this vision will never be fulfilled by secular governments but only as people learn the ways of the Lord and walk in his paths.

Peace: brought about at a cost

Centuries passed, with Isaiah and Micah's visions remaining an unrealised dream. The people of Israel staggered from one episode of conflict to another, and were deprived of peace both when they were in their own homeland and when in exile in Babylon. If outward circumstances seemed relatively beneficial, as they were eventually to prove in exile, there was still the inner turmoil and heartache of remembering Jerusalem from afar, which caused them to weep by the rivers of Babylon (Psalm 137:1). On returning home, the internal factions mounted and disputes arose as to how to respond to those who continued to cause them grief. Peace was denied on every side.

Yet the hope of peace refused to be silenced. The people prayed in their synagogues, 'May he who makes shalom in his High Heaven grant shalom to us.' While the prophets kept the improbable vision alive, it increasingly came to focus on the coming of one who would be the 'Prince of Peace', the Messiah. He, they trusted, would install a government that would be great and of his peace there would be no end (Isaiah 9:6–7). Jesus was that Prince of Peace. At his birth Zechariah rejoiced that he would 'guide our feet into the path of peace' (Luke 1:79), and the angels celebrated the coming of peace on earth (2:13–14). Throughout his life he brought peace to those whose lives to that point had known nothing but trouble. His peace, as he told the disciples, was of a different kind and quality from what they could ever experience elsewhere, a peace that would keep them through the most troubling of circumstances (John 14:27; 16:33).

Many attempts at peace quickly fall apart, as history relentlessly demonstrates. That is often because it is not peace combined with justice but peace that seeks a compromise, usually in a form of ambiguous wording that satisfies everyone and solves nothing at the same time. It is peace of the lowest common denominator variety and fails to convince anyone beyond the printing of the official statement. But the peace Christ offers goes to the root of the problem and deals with its cause, once and for all. He embraces the wickedness and injustice of the all-too-human creatures who live on earth and equally of the invisible powers in the unseen world. In dying, he gives them what they want. There is nothing more that they can seek. In the death of the creator, the Son of God, they have it all. Unlike any tornado chaser, Jesus did not merely chase the multi-vortex of evil at the centre of the spiritual conflict but entered it, allowing it to toss him around horrendously and kill him, only for him to come back to life again. He stilled the eternal storm, just as he had once stilled the storm of the Lake of Galilee, although on a somewhat different scale. He stilled the storm at the cost of his own life, only to reclaim that life again. For his justice triumphs over all injustices, his righteousness pays all the debts of unrighteousness, his power subdues all opposition, and his goodness cancels out the sins of others.

Jesus brings peace as no other did or can bring. He's no mindfulness coach, no relaxation specialist, no psychological therapist, no pain-reducing drug. He came with a message of peace and he came to bring genuine peace to many lives. When the early Christians reflected on this and added his cross and empty tomb into the picture, they realised they had to say something far more profound about Jesus and peace than merely that he taught it, or brought it, or left it as a legacy for his first disciples. They said quite simply, 'He himself is our peace' (Ephesians 2:14).

Peace: brought down to earth

In Christ we have the benefit of tasting the peace that he brought about. We're only on the starter course, as it were. The main course is yet to come, but we already have 'peace with God' through him and that's the key issue (Romans 5:1).

The blessings of God are never for our private enjoyment and it's not surprising that Jesus makes it clear to his disciples that they are to be peacemakers in the world. His logic is simple: peacemaking is the way to be blessed by God and identifies us as his sons and daughters. 'Blessed are the peacemakers, for they will be called children of God' (Matthew 5:9). To be a peacemaker is more than being a peace-lover, especially if that means we enjoy peace but keep it to ourselves, ensuring we are never ruffled or disturbed. To be a peacemaker is more than being a peacekeeper. Peacemakers actively take steps to initiate peace rather than merely trying to keep the lid on things. Thank God for a wide range of folk who have been involved in peacemaking in the name of Christ, whether between black and white in post-apartheid South Africa, between Catholic and Protestant in Northern Ireland, or between native populations and colonists, like the Aborigines and Maoris and the settlers in Australia and New Zealand.

In highlighting that we are called to peace, however, Paul, who mentions this calling twice, has something rather closer to home in mind. The peace he calls for is peace within the local church, between fellow church members. That old ditty puts its finger on it:

To love the world to me's no chore,
My big trouble's the man next door.

The call to peace is not to be professionalised so that it is something one does to people who need to be reconciled some distance from home, resulting in our joining the international jet-setting industry of peacemakers who go from conference to conference and hotel to hotel, often without getting their hands dirty and without result. That can be escapism. No, inherent in our Christian calling is the call to live in peace in our families and with our fellow Christians within the community where we live and worship.

Paul and a mixed marriage

In 1 Corinthians 7:15–16, Paul deals with the situation in which a non-Christian wishes to separate from their Christian spouse, presumably because of their newly acquired faith. Christian purists might wish to cite Jesus' teaching on divorce and the lifelong commitment entailed in the marriage promises. They might want to insist that the Christian partner resists separation at all costs. All that is valid, but Paul says we are not to stand on our rights, belligerently oppose the wishes of our unbelieving partner, and prove awkward and obstructive out of a distorted sense of righteousness. In these circumstances Christians are not bound by the marriage law so much as by the law of peace. So, painful though it may be and reluctant as we might be, as wisely as we can do it, separation is permitted. Peace is more important than tying an unbeliever who doesn't have any commitment to the Christian's moral code to behave in a way they do not want. Divorce is still less than God's ideal, but in the circumstances it may be the lesser of two evils.

Paul and a mixed church

That's a common enough scenario, but the second time Paul reminds us we are called to peace the situation is even more common. Unity in the Christian church is a very fragile thing. We've different spiritual backgrounds; we're all such different personalities; we have such different gifts; we probably have different testimonies about God's dealing with us and emphasise different perspectives on the gospel; we've different levels of education and different amounts of money in our banks; we may be committed to different ways of mission or have different passions about the work Christians should undertake. It's no wonder there are tensions from time to time! There are bound to be disagreements.

Underneath all these causes of our disagreements, however, is another one, a more fundamental one. We still feel the influence of sin. We easily turn unintended slights into long-term resentments, or hold people to account for wrongs done to us long after the offence has been forgotten. I knew a woman who would only enter the church through a certain door in case she met someone who had offended her 20 years before, and then she sat at the diagonally opposite corner of the large and well-attended church so they didn't have to speak to each other. How they could sit at the Lord's Table together I don't know, and, despite my entreaties as their pastor, the feud continued to simmer. I know churches where there have been disputes literally over teacups and sugar bowls. I kid you not! Many more have engaged in worship wars. Noisy children in church and different views regarding youth work are common causes of division. And all those tensions are before we start on anything that might be more serious or doctrinal, like disputes over people's views of the second coming of Christ, or the authority of women in the church.

Unbelievably, in some churches, the hurts, conflicts and accusations are passed down the generations and have become institutionalised. It's what James talked about when he said fights and quarrels in the church arose 'from your desires that battle within you' and why his readers didn't get any answers to their prayers. First, they didn't pray, so how could they expect answers? Secondly, when they did, they prayed with such wrong motives that God would never grant them what they wanted (James 4:1–3).

We don't know precisely what was going on in the church at Colossae, but the reports Paul received made him urge them to 'let the peace of Christ rule in your hearts, since as members of one body you were called to peace. And be thankful' (Colossians 3:15).[41]

His encouragement has often been misunderstood. The peace of Christ ruling *in our hearts* is not about internal serenity or tranquillity: 'We feel at peace inside, no matter what's happening elsewhere. That's all that matters.' No, the reference to the heart is a call for peace to be genuine and a deep-down commitment. The peace Paul is talking about is not peace within but peace between, peace in our relationships. That's plain from the following words that speak of being 'members of one body'. Peace with others is Paul's focus.

How then can we 'let the peace of Christ rule'? There are lots of helpful contemporary programmes and books to assist churches in resolving conflicts. They often enable people to hear each other in a way they haven't been doing. They teach how to communicate using more constructive language. They encourage people to focus on issues rather than personalities. They work towards ensuring that all are treated with dignity and none are victimised. In some conflict situations, especially severe ones, these can prove very beneficial in our pursuing the calling to peace.

Sometimes, however, we might turn too quickly to contemporary techniques of conflict resolution. Contemporary methods may sometimes be just what's needed. But sometimes those methods are just not deep enough and can lead to compromise rather than true transformation and resolution. They may resolve things superficially but leave the real issue untouched. The real issue is that we remain sinners who are not yet fully changed into the image of Christ. It's plain old sinful behaviour that needs addressing.

The training course in peace which Paul offers in Colossians deals with this real issue. What he has written should be the place to start, rather than coming to it when other approaches have been tried and found wanting. I'm not naive. I know it's often complicated. I know we're sensitive to power dimensions in conflicts in a way that previous generations weren't. I know it takes both sides to be reconciled in order that true peace might be experienced. But let's not kill the call to peace through death by a thousand qualifications. Let the Bible speak.

The verses around Paul's insistence that we are 'called to peace' explain how we might begin to put it into operation in our relationships. They tell us to…

- discard sinful attitudes: 'Put to death… rid yourselves of… [take] off your old self…' (3:5–9);
- imitate Christ's character: 'compassion, kindness, humility, gentleness and patience' (3:12–14);
- practise forgiveness often: 'as the Lord forgave you' (3:13);
- embrace God's word: 'Let the message of Christ dwell among you richly' (3:16);
- speak with each other wisely: 'with all wisdom' (3:16);
- enter worship genuinely: 'singing to God with gratitude in your hearts' (3:16);
- live in all things for Jesus: 'whatever you do… do it all in the name of the Lord Jesus' (3:17).

We'll only do that, of course, if we really understand that peace is not an optional extra for the super-Christian but a fundamental aspect of our calling. We are called to serve the Prince of Peace whose kingdom 'is not a matter of eating or drinking [items of dispute and conflict in the early church], but of righteousness, *peace* and joy in the Holy Spirit' (Romans 14:17, emphasis mine). How can we do other than live at peace? To do so is to be a showcase of the gospel of reconciliation we preach to a divided world. To do so is to be a free sample of the kingdom of peace that is yet to come. Peaceful relations are not optional, but inherent in our calling in Christ.

Key lesson

God calls me not to live in a cloud of vague or theoretical peace but in down-to-earth, genuine peace with my fellow church members.

Questions

1. What do people fall out about in the local church? How many of the issues really matter when seen from the viewpoint of the kingdom of God?
2. Think about a conflict situation in your local church, perhaps even one in which you are involved. What do you think Paul would be saying to the factions who are fighting each other?
3. How, and in what situations, can you be a peacemaker, demonstrating you are your Father's child?

8

Called to suffering

To this you were called, because Christ suffered for you, leaving you an example, that you should follow in his steps.
1 PETER 2:21

Any public relations guru advising Peter on how to grow the church would have suggested he should omit half the things he wrote in his first letter. They weren't good news. What made him think that telling his readers they were called to suffering would attract new converts, or even be a wise pastoral thing to say to existing believers who were struggling to maintain their faith? Yet he makes no attempt to hide reality and he candidly admits that suffering is their lot, even when the suffering is unjust.

It may have been that he was summoning up the heroic spirit, as Churchill famously did on 10 May 1940, when he had just become Prime Minister during the Second World War. He had, he said, nothing to offer 'but blood, toil, tears and sweat'. Politicians and people alike rallied to him and to the cause, and the fight against Nazism was galvanised with fresh energy. Is that what Peter is doing? I suggest not.

Looking at suffering from a different angle

As a disciple of Jesus, Peter had learned some deep lessons from his Master, even if they took some time to register. Bearing suffering was at the heart of his Master's mission. At first neither Peter nor his fellow disciples could understand it. When Jesus announced that he must 'suffer many things… and that he must be killed' (Matthew 16:21). Peter naturally argued with him. It was ridiculous. This was not the way God would establish his kingdom. How could people ever object to the most beautiful life and the most loving man that had ever been, let alone seek to dispose of him? Peter was adamant: 'Never, Lord!... This shall never happen to you!' (v. 22). It was crazy to think as Jesus did. Yet, if Peter was adamant, Jesus was even more so. Just moments earlier, Jesus had lauded Peter as 'blessed' and as the rock of the church, because he had declared Jesus to be the Messiah. Now he was rebuking him in the harshest of ways and calling him Satan.

The lesson Jesus delivered that day was the total reverse of conventional wisdom and it took some time to be understood and for its implications to be worked out. Nonetheless, it had imprinted itself deeply on Peter's mind. It made Peter totally reconstruct his worldview, and with it he re-evaluated suffering. So, as an elderly apostle, Peter is able to advise his readers that since we follow a suffering Messiah, we too are called to suffering. If you want to avoid suffering, follow a different Master.

The many faces of suffering

Suffering is a common experience and all of us will be touched by it eventually. Our lot in life is to suffer. It remains, though, a puzzle and an enigma, however much a part of human experience it is. Why does a good and powerful God permit it? Why doesn't he simply eradicate it?

The Bible devotes a good deal of space to the conundrum. Esther tragically illustrates it. Job ponders it but never really resolves it. The Psalms and Lamentations give voice to it. Proverbs teaches us how to minimise it. Ecclesiastes boldly claims there is no answer to it.

Peter adds his own distinctive voice to the conversation and tells us that suffering is not just our unfortunate lot but our special calling in Christ. He does not say everything there is to be said about suffering, but what he does say is arresting and shaped by his own experience and that of his readers.

We can only speculate about the situation his readers were in. It's unlikely that they faced outright persecution but, even so, life seems to have been full of affliction and distress. Peter uses a rich vocabulary in addressing it. He speaks of trials and testing, suffering, physical beatings, threats, slander, 'the fiery ordeal that has come on you' (1 Peter 4:12), being reviled and, after all that, facing the judgement to come. This is not random suffering. Much of it is targeted suffering, not just part of the furniture of life. They're suffering mainly because they are Christians, even if not all of it falls under that label. As 'exiles' they might well be suffering because they are at the bottom of the social and economic heap. As servants they may have suffered unjust whippings. For the most part Peter isn't dealing with the sort of suffering Western Christians are familiar with, that of declining health, or minor inconveniences, or disappointed ambitions, or loss and separation. The early disciples were called to suffering because they were called to Christ. That's the peak that towers through the clouds and provides us with an awesome, captivating sight of faith. Yet, like any mountain summit, there's a path up to it and a path down the other side and, before we reach the peak, which is revealed in 1 Peter 2:21–25, we'll explore the paths that lead to and away from it.

The values of suffering

Suffering proves faith genuine (1 Peter 1:6; 4:12)

People become followers of Jesus for all sorts of reasons. Some do so out of the purest of motives, but an honest reading of history and missionary experience suggests people's motives are often at least mixed when they are converted. In times gone by it was known that some joined a particular church because they were likely to catch the eye of the mine owner, local landowner, or factory manager if they worshipped together on a Sunday and so get a job or promotion at work. Earlier generations spoke of 'rice Christians', meaning those who became Christians because they would be ensured sufficient rice to feed their families if they did. When Eastern Europe rejected Marxism and became open to the West, many initially became Christians because it gave them a way of owning material possessions like clothes and cars. This isn't cynicism; it's a candid admission of reality.

The same has been true from the earliest days. One reason why Paul advised the church in Ephesus to adopt certain rules in supporting widows was that the charity of the early church was being abused (see 1 Timothy 5:9–16).

Peter suggests that one of the values of suffering is that it weeds out those who are not genuine about their faith. Unless people really were committed to being followers of Jesus, the various trials they faced would soon put them off. Why bother continuing in the faith if all you meet is trouble and grief—unless, that is, you really believe in it and have really experienced the grace of God in your life? These ordeals, Peter says, have 'come on you to test you' (4:12). In some measure, suffering is the quality control mechanism of the faith which sorts out the genuine from the free riders who are only in it for what they can get out of it in the here and now.

Joni Eareckson Tada was a vibrant Christian when she suffered a diving accident at the age of 17, in 1967, which left her a wheelchair-bound quadriplegic who was unable to use her hands. Consequently no one can accuse her of not understanding when she writes about suffering. In her book, *A Step Further*, she reflects on it in a way that dovetails with Peter's argument:

> God has shown one of the most effective ways in which suffering can bring glory to Himself—it demonstrates His ability to maintain the loyalty of His people even when they face difficult trials. If being a Christian had brought us nothing but ease and comfort, the world wouldn't learn anything very impressive about God. 'Big deal,' men would say. 'Anyone can get a following by waiting on people hand and foot.' But when a Christian shows faith and love for his Maker in spite of the fact that on the surface, it looks as if he's been forgotten, it does say something impressive. It

shows the scoffers that our God is worth serving even when the going gets tough. It lets the skeptical world know that what the Christian has is real.[42]

Suffering produces spiritual refinement (1 Peter 1:7; 4:1)

When we're flying on an aircraft, we're glad the metals from which it has been made have been subjected to testing. They will have been put through all sorts of stress tests to see if they are safe in a whole range of potentially catastrophic situations. We wouldn't be so keen to fly if the testing had not given us assurance about the quality of the materials from which the plane is made. When it comes to humans, testing not only measures quality but also is a means of refinement, of improving, of learning. Why are soldiers put through those gruelling tests in their training? Partly so that those who are likely to fail in a battle situation can be removed before they are sent to the battlefront and so endanger neither themselves nor the lives of others. But it is also partly to strengthen the recruit, to enable them to develop and achieve levels of fitness and preparedness they would never have reached in the beginning. It's educational, although the recruit may not feel that at the time. A smooth, cosy, easy, trouble-free, laid-back Christian life which has never encountered difficulty or been toughened up is likely to be a shallow Christian life that lacks conviction and fails at the crucial moment.

Spiritually, suffering plays the same role. Peter refers to the refining process that takes place to remove imperfections and enhance the purity of gold, and reminds his readers that faith is of far greater value than any gold.

When he returns to the issue, in 4:1, he focuses on the relationship between suffering and sin. Suffering exposes our imperfections, highlights our weaknesses and uncovers our mixed goals and motives, and our reaction to it reveals our true character. It does not do this to discourage and demotivate, but rather to motivate us to strive for greater holiness. Although we will never achieve sinless perfection until 'the day of Christ' (Philippians 1:6; 3:12–14; 1 John 1:8, 9), suffering provides us with the incentive to change and become more like Christ. Suffering may originate from several sources, but this element of suffering originates in our Father's loving heart and he wants nothing but the very best for us. Hebrews 12 speaks of it in terms of fatherly discipline which does not seem pleasant at the time but, when God exercises it, is always 'for our good, in order that we may share in his holiness'. In this context suffering, viewed as discipline, 'produces a harvest of righteousness and peace for those who have been trained by it' (vv. 7–11). Suffering refines us.

Suffering subverts society's values
(1 Peter 2:19–21; 3:17; 4:14–19)[43]

The world of the New Testament was one where people were acutely conscious of their place in the pecking order and where upholding one's honour was paramount. Any personal slight or infringement of one's dignity would lead to reprisals and retribution. Status was to be maintained at all costs. The administration of justice was highly dependent on one's place in the social hierarchy, with different standards and punishments being applied to slaves, free persons and members of the upper strata, and according to gender.

Against this background, Peter's first letter is nothing short of revolutionary. The theme of suffering subverting society's values runs through the letter, popping up above the surface like the green shoots of a richly planted Dutch tulip field in early spring. Peter's readers are of no importance in their human social matrix but in reality they are a chosen people, 'a royal priesthood, a holy nation, God's special possession' (1 Peter 2:9). Jesus is 'the cornerstone' the builders rejected (2:7). They were to submit to authority, not protest against it, and to 'show proper respect to everyone'. The most persuasive apologetic for their beliefs would be found in good, submissive, clean living, not in employing loud and contentious arguments (2:13–17). Non-retaliation and non-self-assertion were to mark the lives of all believers (4:8–11).

Wives were to be known for the beauty of their inner spirit and be indifferent to jewellery, costumes, cosmetics and coiffure, the usual measures of status then and now (3:1–4). Equally, husbands were not to assert their authority over their wives, but to treat them with respect (3:7).[44] Church elders, who would have been in a position of honour, were not to behave as leaders in other societies and associations would, but be eager to serve, rather than to be served (5:1–4).

The idea of subverting society's values is brought into the sharpest focus when it comes to suffering, as the verses in the subheading above indicate. Slaves had been truly set free by Christ, but while still on this earth they were to submit to their human masters, at all times, even when their masters were unjust and harsh. They, of course, were to avoid meriting punishment because they had done wrong, but they were to accept punishment even when it was unmerited, trusting themselves to God the judge to sort it out. Suffering for doing good might not have been right, but God would be with them in it. Suffering for the name of Christ had an even deeper spiritual value, to which we'll come.

In it all, the believer's reaction to suffering demonstrated their true worldview. To protest, demand one's rights and insist on justice now was exactly how the contemporary culture, revolving as it did around the axis of honour and shame, would function. To accept suffering, particularly if it was unjust or provoked by one's faith in Christ, subverted mainstream cultural values. It was an indication that they had committed 'themselves to their faithful Creator' (4:19). He would not let them down and he would serve ultimate and eternal justice in the end.

Suffering signposts the new age (1 Peter 4:12–17)

That leads us to focus on the relationship between suffering and the coming judgement, as Peter does. In a curious way, Peter argues, the fact that believers experience suffering now is confirmation of a greater judgement to come. We may not immediately appreciate his argument, since again it seems a bit cross-eyed. In fact, he's drawing on a well-worn Jewish belief that Israel would experience a purifying judgement as a preparation for the judgement of the Gentiles. Peter adopts and adapts the idea for the Christians. The suffering that Christians are undergoing is a prelude to the universal act of judgement that all will experience at the end of time.

The fact that Christians are suffering human judgement now, for their faith, is only a beginning. Since Christians are not exempt from suffering, how do evildoers and those 'who do not obey the gospel of God' but reject God's grace and live their own self-serving lives expect to escape judgement? If there really is no judgement, then surely Christians wouldn't be subject to it now. The fact that they are is an indication that they're in the first act of a play, as it were, which is not yet over but whose final act will follow soon. In this paradoxical way, therefore, their suffering serves as a signpost to a reality all men and women will encounter in the future. If people were wise they'd see the direction in which the signpost is pointing and get ready.

Suffering engenders global solidarity (1 Peter 5:9)

On a totally different level, the suffering of Peter's readers in Asia Minor brings them close to other Christians around the globe. 'The family of believers throughout the world is undergoing the same kind of sufferings,' he claims. Indeed they were. The default position of the church then, as it is now, tended to be that of suffering. It is the contemporary Western church which is unusual in enjoying peace and privilege. Even though some present-day Christians in Europe and the USA feel under threat as the church has undoubtedly been marginalised since the 1960s, and even though much contemporary legislation seeks to enshrine secular law which is inclusive of all and discriminates against none (thereby inadvertently, it seems, often discriminating against active believers), the truth is the church in the West remains in a comfortable and fairly secure position.

It's very different elsewhere, where the normal experience of Christians is that of persecution. Until 1990 communist regimes posed many obstacles to Christians practising their faith, including periods of intense persecution. In some post-communist countries the legacy of this remains active. But it is Muslim countries that are now highly restrictive as far as freedom of religion is concerned and intolerant of Christians living out their faith. Statistics of martyrs and those persecuted are notoriously difficult to calculate with any certainty. But, according to the respected Pew Foundation, 70 percent of Christians live in an intolerant environment with many having to flee their homes or made to be outcasts in their own society. And, however one calculates it, the number of those martyred for their loyalty to Jesus Christ runs into thousands.[45]

Suffering is part of the DNA of Christian discipleship, and any suffering (usually, in reality in the West it is no more than a minor inconvenience) we endure leads us closer to those around the world who really do suffer for their allegiance to Jesus as their Lord.

Suffering points to coming glory (1 Peter 4:13–14; 5:1)

Just as suffering points to the coming judgement, so it also points to the coming glory. Believers have already begun to taste God's glory in their lives, since 'the Spirit of glory and of God rests on you'. Suffering is not opposed to God's blessing on one's life, but may be the means to it. For all that, however, it is clear that there is more to come and Peter speaks twice about the glory which is 'to be revealed' in the future. When God's glory is fully revealed believers will be vindicated, their true identity, which is currently hidden (Colossians 3:4), will be made plain, their persecutors will be judged, their suffering will be ended and their reward will be received. So, suffering 'stimulates hope. The spread of persecution and trials points to the nearness of the consummation. The promised land is in sight.'[46]

Suffering as identification with Christ

None of the items in the above list which itemises the value of suffering is persuasive on its own. It would seem as if there is some missing clue which makes sense of them all, as indeed there is. The real heart of Peter's teaching about suffering is found when he connects it all to Jesus. What suffering does, if we react to it in the right way, is to create a closer bond between the disciple and their Lord.

Jesus and his example (1 Peter 2:21–25)

The death of Jesus was much more than an example. It was a decisive event that effected a change and permitted a holy God to forgive sin and welcome rebellious creatures to be reconciled to him. Yet, at the same time, it was also an example. His followers are called to imitate him in their response to suffering.

In a moving passage that builds on Isaiah 53, Peter meditates on the trial and crucifixion of Christ, whom he describes as a sinless ('He committed no sin'), silent ('he did not retaliate… he made no threats'), submissive ('he entrusted himself to' God) saviour ('he himself bore our sins… so that we might die to sin and live for righteousness'). It is because he died that we may live. Likewise, although on a more minor scale, our bearing of suffering can be the means of channelling God's grace to others.

Jesus and his trusting (1 Peter 2:23; 4:19)

In saying all this, Peter is particularly keen to emphasise that in the midst of injustice and undeserved cruelty, Jesus 'entrusted himself to him who judges justly'. Good teachers know they may need to repeat themselves (albeit not too often!) before the penny drops, and Peter does exactly that when he returns to the point in 4:19. He writes, 'those who suffer… should commit themselves to their faithful Creator and continue to do good'. Entrusting our lives to God, no matter what occurs in them, is the right thing to do. Rather than being so concerned about our rights and rather than being angrily self-assertive as so many will be, faith in God is the path to a peace and patience which, in itself, becomes a powerful testimony to the gospel of Jesus Christ.

Furthermore, it is in trusting when we face pain or bewilderment that we discover a greater depth in our relationship with God. The late Elisabeth Elliot, whose husband, Jim, was killed by a tribe of indigenous South American people to whom he was seeking to bring the good news of Jesus, spoke for many Christians when she wrote, 'I am not a theologian or a scholar, but I am very aware that pain is necessary to us all. In my own life, I think I can honestly say that out of the deepest pain has come the strongest conviction of the presence of God and the love of God.'[47]

Paul Mallard, in whose book, *Invest Your Suffering*, I read the quote from Elisabeth Elliot, is no stranger to suffering himself. For over 20 years Edrie, his wife, has been disabled, in spite of which they have gone on touching many lives for Christ through their local and itinerant ministries. In his reflections on their experiences, which at times are written with raw emotion, he tells of an episode which turns out to be a parable. After one bout of hospital treatment the young people in their church presented them with a gift, as only young people could, which was to send them on a hot air balloon ride over Bath. Naively Paul asked the pilot in which direction they would travel, only to be told he had no idea because they were totally dependent on the wind for the speed and direction of their travel. Back on the ground, Paul reflected that just as they had put their lives in the hands of the airstream, and had put their lives in the hands of the hospital, whose medical staff by now had exhausted what they could offer, so they could do no other than place their lives in the hands of God. He writes,

> ... our future was entirely in his hands. This future is unknown terrain, and like our balloon at the mercy of the wind, we have to go in the direction and at the pace that God takes us. Faith involves handing our future to God. We surrender to our heavenly Father, trusting him to take care of our journey. Just because

the wind might have taken us in a direction we didn't expect or anticipate was no reason to stop trusting.[48]

Indeed, for all the tears, Paul and Edrie have discovered, as have countless Christians, that placing our lives in his hands is to put them into the safest place of all. God is worth trusting.

Jesus and the Messiah's woes (1 Peter 4:12–19)

Underlying Peter's writing about suffering there may be the common Jewish idea that God's people would undergo a period of intense suffering before the coming of the Messiah. Peter may be hinting at this when he uses the language about 'the fiery ordeal' and coming judgement, as well as in the general thrust of his argument and its orientation to the future.[49] If so, the suffering of believers is not incidental to the coming of judgement and glory but integral to it, just as is the suffering of the Messiah himself. So, 'the sufferings of Jesus and his followers together constitute the birth pangs through which the new age emerges'.[50] This explains why Peter tells his readers that they are to 'rejoice inasmuch as you participate in the sufferings of Christ'. Suffering as a Christian is more than following in Christ's footsteps, more than copying his example; it is to participate in him, to unite with him at the deepest level.

Jesus and the mark of belonging (1 Peter 4:16)

I've a drawer full of badges I've been given on various occasions to identify myself at conferences and events. Some are even colour-coded for security purposes, so that stewards can immediately see what part I'm playing and where I should, or should not, be permitted to go.

Peter refers to his readers as 'Christians'—a word which is common now but which is very rarely used in the New Testament and was coined by Gentiles to describe who this new Jewish religious sect were. The name on their badges identified them as belonging to Christ. But if 'Christian' was their name, the badge was only ever issued in one colour: the colour of suffering. There is only one Christ the Lord and he is Christ crucified (1 Corinthians 2:2). Suffering, then, assuming they were suffering for the right reasons and not because they had done wrong, marked them out as belonging to the crucified Messiah.

When Peter explains suffering in these terms, it is easier to see why he says we are called to it. Some of Peter's readers were surprised that they were suffering (1 Peter 4:12). Presumably they thought that once they became followers of Jesus, the Lord of all, they would be kept safe and his powerful Spirit would protect them from it. Yet their suffering not only continued but was compounded because now, in addition to any run-of-the-mill injustices they would daily bear as slaves, they were persecuted because they were Christians. What was that all about? Their thinking needed to be grounded on a better foundation. Who was the Lord whom they had come to trust? The Son of Man who was crucified under Pontius Pilate. To follow him inevitably meant suffering. To unite with him meant that sharing in his sufferings was unavoidable.

Perhaps now we can see why Peter does not describe suffering as an unfortunate circumstance to be avoided if possible, or the result of conflict which will catch some in the crossfire, or the privilege of a select few virtuoso Christians. It is a calling incumbent on all who 'bear his name'.

Key lesson
'Consider it pure joy, my brothers and sisters, whenever you face trials of many kinds because…' (James 1:2)

Questions
1. How do you naturally understand or react to suffering? How much does Peter's teaching about suffering act as a corrective to your understanding?
2. How far do our Christian attitudes to suffering and death subvert the normal attitudes of our culture, or do we merely mirror them?

3. What awareness do we have of the suffering church around the world? What can we do to support 'the family of believers' who are persecuted?
4. Could people identify us as Christians by our response to life's circumstances?

9

Called to hope

... the hope to which he has called you.
EPHESIANS 1:18

... just as you were called to one hope when you were called.
EPHESIANS 4:4

On 5 August 2012, a rockfall at the San José mine in the Atacama Desert, Chile, trapped 33 miners deep underground. The rescue operation proved enormously difficult and there was no guarantee of success. Relatives and friends flocked to the site and set up a camp to watch and wait. They named it 'Camp Hope'. It was to be mid-October before their hope was realised and all 33 came out alive and, given their ordeal, in good health.

Hope is one of the most universal qualities of humanity. It is an amazingly resilient characteristic of human beings, exercised in the most despairing of circumstances and held on to when reason would often suggest it is foolish. Refugees in miserable camps, patients facing terminal illnesses, the hungry facing failed harvests, shanty-town dwellers facing bleak prospects, parents nursing a sick and fragile baby, an unemployed person staring into a grim future; all exercise hope. Hope endures. Hope orients people towards the future and, to quote the sociologist Peter Berger, they have 'an unconquerable propensity to hope for the future'.[51] Take hope away and life shrivels and dies.

Given this, it is not surprising that the gospel of Jesus Christ has a lot to say about hope. Paul, writing to the Ephesians, can say to them not once but twice that they were called to hope. Christians belong to a body of hopeful people, although, admittedly, you wouldn't always see that in the average Western church, which can be angst-ridden, problem-filled and downcast in vision. Rightly burdened by the problems of the world, it's too easy for despair to push the hope of the gospel to the margins of faith. Biblical Christianity, however, makes hope central.

What is hope?

Hope can easily be mistaken for the kind of wishful thinking that is based on sheer fantasy. I've visited more than one terminally ill patient in hospital whose family conspire with them to deny the inevitable onset of death and pretend they'll soon be home and all will be well again. I understand why people do this, because believing the denial rather than facing the reality may give the sick person strength. More often, though, it is foolish and one can see the family clumsily play-acting with each other as they try to avoid facing the truth. The effect may well be that the patient is denied the opportunity of dying well, saying goodbye properly, setting their affairs in order, and preparing to meet God. Genuine hope is not a delusion. Genuine hope is a well-placed, well-founded belief, based on solid truth, that we can be sure of a particular future outcome even though we have not yet experienced it.

When flying back from a visit overseas, I have often looked forward with hope to my wife greeting me at the airport and driving me home. As I come in to land I know my expectation is a genuine hope and not a mere empty wish. I know she will be there for several reasons: we've arranged it; she keeps her promises; she has met me many times before; she longs to see me again (no, really!). I believe that she will be there and the evidence supports it. Yet, since I have not yet seen her in person, since I have not yet landed, collected my bags, gone through customs and come out to the agreed meeting point, my hope is still a hope. It is not yet something I have actually experienced. It only becomes a reality when I see her face to face and greet her with hugs and kisses.

Hope points to a future reality that we have not yet experienced, but to a future reality which is built on a solid foundation. It is not delusional, mere wishful thinking, or denial of the facts.

What is 'the hope to which he has called you'?

Future inheritance (Ephesians 1:18–19)

Paul defines the hope to which the Ephesians were called as 'the riches of his glorious inheritance in his holy people, and his incomparably great power for us who believe'. What we have already begun to experience of God's grace, which is already 'lavished on us' (Ephesians 1:8), will one day be even more lavishly experienced. As the veteran theologian J.I. Packer commented in a recent interview, 'This [inheritance] is something we begin to experience here; I don't think we get very far with it, frankly, compared with how it is going to be in the world to come.'[52] It is as if the child of wealthy parents, who has been generously provided for while the parents are alive, on their death at last fully receives their inheritance and realises how little knowledge they had of the wealth, property and possessions that would become theirs. Whatever they had received up till then was a fraction of what would one day be theirs. Paul's language is stretched to the limits. This inheritance is abundant in its riches, glorious in its quality and powerful in its impact in delivering full and final salvation.

The result of all this, as Paul reminded the Corinthians, is that 'our light and momentary troubles are achieving for us an eternal glory that far outweighs them all' (2 Corinthians 4:17). To enter into that inheritance requires faithful perseverance, and faithful perseverance requires hope as its motivating and sustaining power.

The inheritance to which we look forward is not simply personal. The inheritance is shared 'in his holy people', and even more than this has cosmic implications. For, on the day when Christ returns and signals that his people are entering into their inheritance, the creation itself will be transformed. In Ephesians, Paul speaks about the times reaching their fulfilment, when all things in heaven and on earth will be brought into unity under Christ (1:10; see also Romans 8:19–21; 1 Corinthians 15:24–28; Colossians 1:20). In other words, the current disjointedness of creation will be brought to an end and creation will be brought back under God's righteous control to serve his loving purposes. The effects of sin will be over. Evil will be banished. Eden will be restored and the cosmos healed because everything will be in its right place under Christ and in its right relationship with God. The devastating effects of earthquake and tsunamis, the horror of famine and the devastation of war, the barrenness of the earth and the destructiveness of the forces of nature will be at an end. Such is our hope.

Present unity (Ephesians 4:4)

On the second occasion when Paul reminds the Ephesians that they have been called to hope he remarks that they had been 'called to *one* hope'. Reading between the lines, there were tensions in the church at Ephesus that resulted in some measure of disunity. Unity in their faith was something that they still had to reach for (Ephesians 4:13). It was a work in progress. The causes of the tensions were complex, including, perhaps, the fact that members of the church all exercised different gifts and felt their gifts were more important than anyone else's in the church (4:11–12).[53] But two factors contributed to their fractious relationships. The first was the plain old-fashioned sin of self-centredness. They lacked humility and gentleness with each other (4:2) and were behaving like immature infants rather than grown-up Christians (vv. 14–16). How many churches still, one wonders, tolerate 'teenage' tantrums among their members instead of challenging such immature behaviour with loving robustness, so that the gospel of God is not dishonoured by disunity? They were not called to different hopes, but to one hope, and the effect of their all sharing this one hope was to be seen in their behaviour towards each other and their unity.

The second major reason for possible tensions in the church in Ephesus was the fact that they were a mixed church, made up of Jews and Gentiles. The division between these two great ethnic groups was a major chasm that ran through every part of the ancient world, including its social, political and religious dimensions. Spanning it was like spanning the Grand Canyon, and the early church did not always do so successfully. Yet, Jew and Gentile alike had been called to *one* hope, not two different hopes.

Earlier Paul described the Gentiles as those 'without hope' (Ephesians 2:12). Now they shared the same hope that the Jews had. Not all Jewish believers in Christ readily understood and accepted that.[54] The Jewish way, some felt, with its continuing reliance on their law and customs, made them first-class citizens in God's new society, whereas the Gentiles were second-rate, travelling to their future inheritance in economy class. Paul is adamant. There was only one way God would rescue anyone and that was not because of their national and religious heritage, not because of their acceptance of certain customs and laws, but simply through their having faith in the grace he had made available through Christ (2:8–10). There was only one road to God, not two. There was only one hope, not two. How then could they be a divided people?

The force of Paul's argument should not be lost on us, even though we belong to an overwhelmingly Gentile church, where the precise form of the original division hardly appears on our radar screens. Nonetheless, we are often unaware of subtle new distinctions that can contribute to divisions within local churches. In some places it is locals versus incomers that proves to be the fault line. In others, it's those who grew up in the church and were socialised through the Sunday school into the faith versus those who are converted with no church background, have no clue how to 'behave' in church and sometimes bring a pile of moral or emotional baggage with them. In yet other places, the church still operates on the basis of class or ethnic divisions. In still other local churches the different denominational backgrounds of its members can cause a crack that can break open with damaging effects when least expected.

In all these situations, we need to grasp that whatever our differences, our calling is to *one* hope. As a result, we are compelled to speak 'the truth in love' and 'grow to become in every respect the mature body of him who is the head, that is, Christ'. For 'from him the whole body, joined and held together by every supporting ligament, grows and builds itself up in love, as each part does its work' (Ephesians 4:15–16).

What does hope do?

Andrew Fuller, the pastor-theologian who served as the first secretary of the Baptist Missionary Society, wrote,

> Hope, or *an expectation of future good*… is one of the principal springs that keep mankind in motion. It is vigorous, bold and enterprising. It causes men to encounter dangers, endure hardships, and surmount difficulties innumerable, in order to accomplish the desired end. In religion it is of no less consequence… It makes a considerable part of the religion of those that truly fear God.[55]

Hope keeps us going, fuels our perseverance and prevents us from giving up too easily. It replenishes our energies when we're running dry and does so by lifting our eyes from present realities to future prospects.

If anyone needed hope to keep them going it was the Ephesian Christians. The small group of Christ-followers must often have felt intimidated by their surroundings. First, their town was famous as the centre of the worship of the Greek goddess Artemis (or Diana, as she was known in Roman circles). Their whole economy was built around the tourists who came to worship at her temple and buy mementos and trinkets to take back home. Paul's preaching of Jesus, even though he did not denounce her, had sparked a riot as some saw the economic consequences of his gospel (see Acts 19:31–41).[56]

Secondly, Ephesus was a centre for sorcery and the practice of magic arts and spells. The sense of evil supernatural powers was palpable. This was all too evident during Paul's first visit to Ephesus (the story is told in Acts 19:8–20), which is why Luke highlights that 'God did extraordinary miracles through Paul' on this mission (Acts 19:11). Luke tells the amusing story of how when the seven sons of Sceva sought to imitate Paul and hijack the name of Jesus to do supernatural wonders, they met an embarrassing comeuppance. When many people were converted to Christ in Ephesus, they renounced their former practices by publicly burning the scrolls which had served as their textbooks in magic. This explains why Paul gives attention to the nature of spiritual warfare and to the armour with which Christians can equip themselves when he wrote to this church (Ephesians 6:10–20). They knew their lives were not in the hands of blind fate, nor were they fighting ordinary, visible enemies, but they were up 'against the rulers, against the authorities, against the powers of this dark world and against the spiritual forces of evil in the heavenly realms' (Ephesians 6:12).

Like many an inferior army, trapped and facing the impossible odds of superior firepower, they knew everything seemed stacked against them. As with the soldiers at Dunkirk, there was little likelihood of being rescued alive. What they needed to keep them going was hope.

Hope empowers us to keep going when secular culture derides our faith. Hope enables us to persevere even in the face of setbacks. It makes us look forward to a better future. But even if things are going well, hope still has a positive part to play. It prevents us from settling down and being content with things as they are as we strive forward and work for a better future. Søren Kierkegaard defined hope as 'a passion for the possible'.[57] So hope is no 'pie in the sky' escapism but rather is intensely this-worldly in its concerns and practical in its outcomes.

How does hope differ from faith?

Hebrews 11:1 says something very similar to how I defined hope above (although without mentioning my wife!) about faith: 'Now faith is confidence in what we hope for and assurance about what we do not see.' Faith and hope are obviously closely connected. Paul talks of them together on a number of occasions (1 Corinthians 13:13; Galatians 5:5; Colossians 1:5, 23; 1 Thessalonians 1:3; 5:8). They look like two peas in a pod. So how do they differ?

No one has explained it better than Jürgen Moltmann, the German theologian, who wrote in his *Theology of Hope*:

> Thus, faith believes God to be true, hope awaits the time when this truth shall be manifest; faith believes that he is our Father, hope anticipates that he will ever show himself to be a Father towards us; faith believes eternal life has been given to us, hope anticipates that it will sometime be revealed; faith is the foundation upon which hope rests, hope nourishes and sustains faith… Without hope, faith falls to pieces, becomes faint-hearted and ultimately a dead faith. It is through faith that man finds the path of true life, but it is only hope that keeps him on the path…Thus in the Christian life faith has the priority, but hope the primacy.[58]

Add to your faith hope.

The basis of hope

What distinguishes Christian hope from fantasy, from wishful thinking? How can we know our hope is well-founded? The answer is because Christ Jesus is 'our hope' (1 Timothy 1:1). Except for him there might still be a few minor advantages in going to church, since surveys suggest churchgoers are healthier and happier than many, but our faith would in all honesty be futile and our hope delusional. But Jesus changes everything.

In his lifetime he brought hope to many people whose lives had been mired in despair, not by encouraging them to adopt the power of positive thinking but by actually healing them from sickness, releasing them from chains, forgiving them for sins and reconciling them to God. After his death, the apostles point us to a twin focus which is the ground of our hope.

The resurrection of Jesus

Jesus removed the biggest roadblock we face on the road to hope, which takes the shape of the grave. Death seems to be the final full stop in our lives that renders everything to that point worthless—unless there is something beyond the grave of which we can be sure. When Jesus died, many of his disciples thought the dream of God establishing his rule on the earth was over. After Good Friday, they thought they'd woken up to the same grubby, oppressed world as before they'd started to follow Jesus. He had inspired hope, but to what purpose? The forces against him seemed to have conquered and snuffed out hope. But they reached such a despairing conclusion too soon.

Good Friday was followed by Easter Sunday, when the bars of his grave were torn open and death was conquered. Satan had summoned all the forces of darkness against Jesus but they could not overcome him. His light was irrepressible. His life unassailable. His resurrection removed, once and for all, the roadblock to hope and opened the way for us to follow him into the new creation, where God would truly reign unchallenged for ever. Except for that, as Paul says in the expansive passage he writes on this subject to the Corinthians, our faith would be futile, nothing has changed, we're still unforgiven sinners, bearing false witness to the world, and 'are of all people most to be pitied' (1 Corinthians 15:12–19; see the whole passage, 15:1–58).

Some Christians get very excited about the testimonies of those who have near-death experiences and think that in that moment before they return to life on earth they have a glimpse of heaven. I've no expertise to help me judge the veracity of such stories, but I do know my hope is not based on them. They cannot add to the basis of my hope. They may be interesting but they are superfluous. I know for sure that Jesus who was put to death under Pontius Pilate rose from the dead three days later and was subsequently seen by many, many witnesses. His one resurrection outweighs any number of near-death experiences, however fascinating they may be. My hope is founded on the empty tomb of Jesus of Nazareth.

The return of Jesus

The second element on which the apostles focus our hope is that 'this same Jesus… will come back' from heaven, his present dwelling place (Acts 1:11). The early Christians patiently waited for 'the blessed hope—the appearing of the glory of our great God and Saviour, Jesus Christ' (Titus 2:13). The story is not over yet. There's another act to come to bring it to completion.

A party of tourists were visiting a museum and were introduced by their guide to a painting of a chess game in which Mephistopheles was holding Faust's king in checkmate. The tourists failed to notice as they went on their way that they'd left one of their number behind, until they suddenly heard the cry, echoing down the corridor, 'It's a lie! It's a lie. The king has another move.' Unknown to them, their fellow tourist was a Russian chess champion who could see what others couldn't. In spite of appearances, the game wasn't over. Faust's king still had another move to make which would break his opponent's seeming victory.[59]

We have hope because our King still has another move. Improbable? Yes. Hard to believe? Yes. But then, so was the fact that God would be embodied among human beings, commencing life as a baby in Bethlehem. So is the fact that an insignificant rabbi from the extreme edge of the Roman Empire would become the Messiah, or that a victim of Roman crucifixion would become Lord of all, and the founder of a great worldwide movement which anticipates the coming day of the new creation. Hope in his return is not misplaced. It is well founded.

So, what do we do in the meantime? 'We hope,' says Paul, 'for what we do not yet have, [so] we wait for it patiently' (Romans 8:25).

> May the God of hope fill you with all joy and peace as you trust in him, so that you may overflow with hope by the power of the Holy Spirit.
> **ROMANS 15:13**

Key lesson
Live in hope and do not be discouraged or despairing, but entrust the future to the Christ who has risen from the dead.

Questions
1. What distinguishes Christian hope from the illusion of hope found among those who do not believe in Jesus?
2. Do you belong to a hopeful church? If so, what are the characteristics of its hope? If not, how can you inject hope into it?
3. Look back and identify times when hope in Christ has kept you going. Did you express thankfulness to God for enabling you to persevere, or did you take his gifts for granted?
4. What do we mean by saying that Jesus is the hope of the world? What impact does it have on our living and communicating the Christian message?

10

Called heavenwards

I press on towards the goal to win the prize for which God has
called me heavenwards in Christ Jesus.
PHILIPPIANS 3:14

A fresh young curate was visiting the house of a dying young man. The
house was suffused with the solemn hallmarks of anticipated grief.
The curtains were drawn and the conversations were whispered. He
bounded up the stairs into the bedroom and burst out, 'I hear you're
dying. How absolutely marvellous.' This story is told of someone who
went on to be an influential bishop,[60] but any ministerial student who
adopted such an approach today would be likely to fail their selection
board! But surely the curate was right—if, that is, we truly believe in the
hope of the resurrection.

I think the curate and the apostle Paul would have seen eye to eye,
at least on this topic. Heaven was very much on Paul's mind as he
languished in a Roman jail, not knowing whether his next steps
would take him to freedom or to execution. Whatever call the Roman
emperor was to make about his case, there was a greater call—the call
heavenwards—that occupied his mind more. Paul's one ambition in
life had been to live for Christ, but he saw dying as a 'gain'. He admits
that dying itself would require some courage; even so, dying would be
a great step forward, not because it meant escaping this life with its
challenges but because it would fulfil his life's ambition. He longed for
the full and uninterrupted union with Christ which death would bring
(Philippians 1:20–26).

Perhaps it was the imminent prospect of death which made Paul
conscious of the pull of heaven, as he is in Philippians 3:14. Perhaps,
though, this call 'heavenwards' isn't quite what we might expect.

Heaven: our destination?

When Paul says he is called heavenwards, is he meaning that heaven is his, and our, ultimate destination and he can't wait to get there? Is it the place where he and we will spend eternity? That's very much the common Christian belief. But to believe that may be something of a distortion of what the New Testament teaches. If we mean by heaven some ethereal reality which is to be found out there somewhere in our incredible cosmos, to which our immortal selves will journey after death (or on the day of resurrection) by courtesy of some form of divine space travel, we may have got it wrong. The vision of the New Testament is never about resurrected souls dwelling in heaven, listening to yet more harp music, as in popular imagination. It is a vision of the creation of a new heaven and a new earth, of a holy city '*coming down out of heaven* from God', with God dwelling among his people, who inhabit their transformed bodies in a newly renovated greater Eden (see Revelation 21:1—22:5; 2 Peter 3:11–13; 1 Corinthians 15:35–57). The destination to which Christians are heading is a renewed creation, not a place that leaves this creation behind on some divine scrapheap.[61]

What we may have pinned our hope on as far as heaven is concerned is true of the new creation to which we are heading. The new creation will be the place of ultimate perfection and authentic reality. We will have left behind the shadowlands of this earth with all the overtones of darkness, fear, frustration, suffering, unreality and hollowness that such a word conjures up. As C.S. Lewis said, 'Joy is the serious business of heaven',[62] or rather of the new creation.

What, then, is heaven? Quite simply heaven is God's dwelling place. That's what we say every time we pray the Lord's Prayer: 'Our Father, who is in heaven' (see Matthew 6:9). John tells us Jesus came down from heaven and has returned to it, for a time, until he completes his work of salvation and judgement (John 3:13, 31; 6:25–58; 12:28; 17:1–5).

Our reward is certainly kept in heaven, and all God's future goodness is stored up there for us (Luke 6:23). But, as Tom Wright points out,

'If I say to a friend "I've kept some beer in the fridge for you", that doesn't mean that he has to get in the fridge in order to drink the beer.'[63] It is the reward that is kept safe there, rather than the place as a final destination, which concerns Paul when he says he is 'called heavenwards'.

Put another way, he's stretching out for the finishing tape. Athletic contests and wrestling tournaments were common in Paul's world and here, as elsewhere (1 Corinthians 9:24–27; Philippians 3:14), he takes up the desire of the contestants to win the prize and applies it to his own Christian life and ministry. He's putting all his energies into reaching out for the winning tape, for the final bell of the contest to be rung, in order that he may gain the reward.

The image is transparent. No athlete, no wrestler, is likely to win unless they undergo training. The training is never a one-off but always a prolonged process that requires perseverance and determination. I have a number of friends who've run a marathon, although I have never been tempted to join them. None of them have just turned up for the event and expected to succeed. All have run regularly, usually starting with shorter distances and building up, until their fitness peaks at just the right time on race day. Their eye is on the sponsor money, on achieving a certain time, and on getting the medal. That is what motivates them. Future reward determines present behaviour and that's what Paul has in mind when he says we are 'called heavenwards'.

Heaven: our orientation

Heaven is not so much our destination as our orientation, the axis which determines the path of our present life. That certainly rings true in terms of the way Paul speaks of it. His life revolves around doing what pleases God. Shortly after Paul speaks of being 'called heavenwards', he says 'our citizenship is in heaven' (Philippians 3:20). Expat Brits may have chosen to live in a sunny climate in an overseas country, but most of them never 'go native'. Most of them take a bit of Britain with them, as is clear from the language they speak, the food they eat, the papers they read, the TV programmes they watch and even the way they dress. Philippi was a colony of Rome. In effect it was a little bit of Rome planted in Asia Minor. We are a colony of heaven planted on earth. We should not be ashamed about living according to the customs and rules of heaven, the place where God dwells, insofar as we can, while here on earth. In fact, that's our calling!

Heaven will be the place where righteousness reigns, so we are called to righteous living now. Heaven is the place where there is no more sin, so we are called to live holy lives now. Heaven is the place where there is no injustice, so we work for justice now. Heaven is the place where there are no tears, so we need to dry the tears of others now. Heaven is the place where there will be no more pain, so we must do what we can to combat suffering in all its forms now. Heaven is the place where there is no more death, so although we will inescapably face physical death, we must ensure that we will not face the 'second death' (Revelation 2:11; 20:6) which is the destiny of those who have not placed their faith in Christ.

This means, as Jürgen Moltmann explains, that:

> This hope makes the Christian Church a constant disturbance in human society [since this world constantly tries to turn itself into a 'continuing city'!]. It makes the church the source of continual new impulses towards the realization of righteousness, freedom and humanity in the light of the promised future that is to come.[64]

For many of us, this life is demanding enough and negotiating our way through it is enough to contend with, without taking into account the next. Our eyes are not fixed on the far horizon but on the near sight of needing to pay the bills, care for the kids, feed the cat and keep the job. Yet, if we were only to lift our eyes, we might be able to put some of these issues in a better perspective.

In one of his most personal and heart-to-heart letters, 2 Corinthians,

Paul sets out what keeps him going as a preacher of the gospel in spite of many setbacks and disappointments, not least with the Corinthian church itself. Using a series of contrasts, he tells them honestly why it is that he doesn't lose heart. He says:

- some may focus on the outward but it's the inward that matters;
- some may focus on troubles but it's glory that's critical;
- some may focus on what is seen but it's the unseen that is real;
- some may focus on the temporary but it's the eternal that counts (2 Corinthians 4:16–18).

To let our lives revolve around the call heavenwards will almost certainly bring the way many of us live—without this eternal perspective—into question. We won't let our ambitions be determined by what society dictates as 'must-haves' or 'success'. We won't get worked up about our children's future education, as if God is not to be trusted. Our anxiety levels may reduce as we learn to live a little less frenetically, even though we're members of a driven society. We won't accept that 'anything goes' morally, since we'll want to be ready to stand before 'the judgment seat of Christ' (2 Corinthians 5:10). We'll know that what he thinks of us is far more significant than what the neighbours, or the boss, or even the mother-in-law thinks. We won't be fooled into thinking that this material world, this playground of pleasure, is the ultimate reality. It isn't. Ultimate reality is where God is.

The early Christians understood this better perhaps than we do. According to the Letter of Mathetes to Diognetus, written possibly around AD130:

> Christians are indistinguishable from other men either by nationality, language or customs. They do not inhabit separate cities of their own, or speak a strange dialect, or follow some outlandish way of life. Their teaching is not based upon reveries inspired by the curiosity of men. Unlike some other people, they champion no purely human doctrine. With regard to dress, food and manner of life in general, they follow the customs of whatever

city they happen to be living in, whether it is Greek or foreign.

And yet there is something extraordinary about their lives. They live in their own countries as though they were only passing through. They play their full role as citizens, but labor under all the disabilities of aliens. Any country can be their homeland, but for them their homeland, wherever it may be, is a foreign country. Like others, they marry and have children, but they do not expose them. They share their meals, but not their wives.

They live in the flesh, but they are not governed by the desires of the flesh. They pass their days upon earth, but they are citizens of heaven. Obedient to the laws, they yet live on a level that transcends the law. Christians love all men, but all men persecute them. Condemned because they are not understood, they are put to death, but raised to life again. They live in poverty, but enrich many; they are totally destitute, but possess an abundance of everything. They suffer dishonour, but that is their glory. They are defamed, but vindicated. A blessing is their answer to abuse, deference their response to insult. For the good they do they receive the punishment of malefactors, but even then they rejoice, as though receiving the gift of life. They are attacked by the Jews as aliens, they are persecuted by the Greeks, yet no one can explain the reason for this hatred.[65]

These Christians knew what it meant to be 'called heavenwards'.

Heaven: our determination

From this perspective, it may seem as if life here is merely a training ground for the next life, but that would certainly be to misunderstand Paul's point. We may be called heavenwards but very much for the purposes of living in a right way while we are earthside. This is more than a boot camp for heaven. How we live now matters. But living aright in the present world in the midst of what Paul described as 'a warped and crooked generation' isn't easy (Philippians 2:15). 'Exactly,' Paul would say, 'don't I know it. That's my point.' To live in a way that fits us for heaven requires determination. The Christian life will not be a leisurely ride in the park but a strenuous race to the winning tape.

Paul confesses that he hasn't arrived yet. He doesn't always respond as perfectly to the call of heaven as he might. Consequently, he says, 'One thing I do: forgetting what is behind and straining towards what is ahead, I press on towards the goal to win the prize for which God has called me heavenwards in Christ Jesus' (Philippians 3:13–14). Two factors are involved if we are to reach our goal—forgetting what's behind and straining towards what's ahead.

Forgetting the past

In forgetting the past, Paul is not suggesting that we should wipe our memory banks of God's past grace and never express gratitude for what has happened in times gone by. He's keen enough on telling his testimony in other places to disprove that, and he never tires of recalling the sense of wonder he felt when he encountered the living Christ on the road to Damascus. Rather, he is saying that we should set ourselves free from anything that would drag us back and prevent us from making progress. These encumbrances might be as much positive as negative. We might look back to 'the glory days', be wedded to great pastors who instructed us and on whom we became dependent, to successful times of ministry, to full churches in times gone by or to past blessings so much that we get stuck there in the past and don't reach out to God for today. But the encumbrances are more likely to be negative and include past failures, habitual sins, earlier discouragements, or disappointments with other Christians. If we are to progress spiritually, as God wants, we must cut loose from these or they'll constantly hold us back.

Straining towards the future

'Straining' towards what's ahead speaks of the determination we'll need to reach the winning tape, the sort of determination we see in an athlete like Mo Farah winning the 5,000 or 10,000 metres' race. Our commitment to the prize of the Christian life compares poorly with the commitment of many who seek to achieve great goals in ordinary life. We prefer a comfortable, easy-going life where the Christian faith serves us rather than we serve it, and which fits conveniently with our other goals. Paul will have none of it. The Christian life is a race which requires effort if it is a genuine faith.

Effort is required because there are plenty of obstacles en route and plenty of counter-forces to drag us back. The Bible often sums them up as 'the world, the flesh and the devil'. The world sets the wrong goals and ambitions in front of us, which John described as 'the lust of the eyes, and the pride of life' (1 John 2:16). In the wider context of the Western world, believers are a tiny minority of people, swimming against the powerful currents of secularism. That takes some effort! The flesh, by which we mean our still-sinful natures that are yet to be fully transformed, drags us back. The devil scatters a number of obstacles on the track to throw us off course. They include his accusations, causing disruption in the church, distracting us from our primary calling, and that old enemy: discouragement. Like John Bunyan's Pilgrim our journey will take us through the Valley of Death, Vanity Fair, Lucre Hill and Doubting Castle. Like the Pilgrim, we'll meet Pliable, World-Wiseman, Talkative, Apollyon and Demas on the way to the Celestial City.[66] The journey will not be easy. Any progress towards the fulfilment of our calling requires resolve and resilience.

That's demanding, but it is not a cause of despair. Paul introduces our calling heavenwards with the words, 'I press on to take hold of that for which Christ Jesus took hold of me' (Philippians 3:12). We do not run towards the winning tape unaided, but empowered by the Christ who has reached out to us and taken hold of us. Picture the small schoolchild running at Sports Day, inspired by the shouts of Mum and Dad who are there at the finishing line urging them on, and you just begin to get the picture. But, alas, it is an inadequate analogy, for God's grip on us and God's Spirit within us are far more gracious, firm and powerful than any pushy parent.

We're not there yet. We must never be complacent in the misplaced confidence that at the end God will change us in 'the twinkling of an eye' (1 Corinthians 15:52), so why bother? Rather, let's join Paul, who is

> not saying that I have this all together, that I have made it. But I am well on the way, reaching out for Christ, who has so wondrously reached out for me. Friends, don't get me wrong: By no means do I count myself an expert in all this, but I've got my eye on the goal, where God is beckoning us onward—to Jesus. I'm off and running, and I'm not turning back.
> PHILIPPIANS 3:12–14, MSG

Key lesson
Keep pressing on with confidence, knowing that God has not finished with you yet.

Questions
1. How do you understand heaven? Is it just the place you go to when you die or does it have any implications for your present life?
2. In what ways may the past be holding you back in your spiritual life?
3. Would you say you were a 'determined' Christian? What would others say about you?
4. Paul speaks of Christ taking hold of him. Can you speak in similar terms and what does such a phrase mean to you?

11

Called according to his purpose

We know that in all things God works for the good of those who love him, who have been called according to his purpose.
ROMANS 8:28

Christians have a number of 'good luck' sayings. Chief among them is: '"For I know the plans I have for you," declares the Lord, "plans to prosper you and not to harm you, plans to give you hope and a future"' (Jeremiah 29:11). These words, scattered around like confetti at a wedding to bless anyone who's finding the going tough or who is unsure of their future, are meant well. Unfortunately scant regard, if any, is paid to the original setting of these words, where God tells a sinful Israel, 'You will... find me when you seek me with all your heart' (29:13). Repentance and obedience would lead to the blessings God longed to give them.

From the New Testament, it is Paul's words in Roman 8:28, 'all things work together for good' (NRSV), that are often wrenched from their setting and sprinkled like a cake decoration to make people feel good. I confess I've been on the receiving end of this verse as pastoral encouragement during some hard times, but it was spoken in the same tone that Job's friends adopted. It was true and orthodox but lacked compassion and sensitive application. It wasn't spoken through gritted teeth but I heard it through gritted ears!

A friend grappling with the grief of his brother's suicide said much the same thing in a recent email. Those words, he said, haven't been a comfort. What has comforted him is the knowledge that although God is silent he is with him in the grief since he similarly lost his own Son in 'a sudden and inexplicable death'. Another friend of mine set out with a clear vision and hopeful expectation of being a missionary in

Africa, but during his first week there he was involved in a car accident that resulted in someone being killed. Not a great start to a career of bringing 'good news' to people! Where was God working for good in that? he rightly wanted to know.

We need to use the words sensitively, even though they are the natural ones to turn to when we're facing exam failure, disappointments, accidents, sudden bereavement and a host of other struggles in life that make us want to cry out, 'Why me?'

It is too easy to reduce this verse to a mere slogan, a piece of worldly wisdom like, 'Cheer up, it may never happen,' or the ubiquitous 'Have a good day.' But its meaning is much deeper and at the heart of it lies the fact that the Christian is 'called according to [God's] purpose'. So let's look at its meaning more deeply using those 'honest serving-men', as Rudyard Kipling called them, which he claimed had taught him all he knew.[67] The use of these very basic questions often unlocks the meaning of a text, and Romans 8:28 is no exception.

1. What?

'All things work together for good' (NRSV)

Every word is of significance. In the flow of what Paul is writing, the 'all things' undoubtedly tends towards the negative and suffering side of experience. 'All things', however, is truly comprehensive and includes not only the rough and tough experiences of life but the pleasant and sunny passages of life as well. It encompasses the routine and humdrum days as much as the extreme days, whether highs or lows. It embraces the mountaintop days of great blessing and the spiritual valleys. It means the wrong decisions we take as well as the right ones. It covers our failures and our sins as well as our spiritual victories and progress. It tells us God is greater than them all and sovereign over them all. He is not limited to working only when conditions are right and people are totally aligned with him, but can work when things are out of joint with him and people out of step with him. Nothing can defeat him. He reigns to achieve his ultimate purposes in it all, whatever we throw at him.

These things, Paul says, 'work together'.[68] They synergise. Just down the road from where I live the Highways Agency is reconstructing a major road junction between two motorways and a busy 'A' road to ensure a safer environment and a smoother flow of traffic. The whole thing has looked a mess for a year or more and has been something of an inconvenience as speed on the main motorway is restricted, as the shape of the road often changes to accommodate the building of new bridges and carriageways, and as mud seems to be taking over! I've not been able to make sense of it for months. Nothing looked as if it was going to connect up or improve anything. But gradually, as the work nears completion, it is all fitting together. The individual elements of the construction have been carefully planned to fit together. We're going to look back and see what was in the planner's eyes all along. And we're going to benefit from the mess and inconvenience of it all as we're heading for the completion of the project.

So it is with God. He takes the individual experiences of our lives, which we often find very difficult to make sense of, and meshes them together into one harmonious and complete project that will make sense one day. I look back on experiences that left me perplexed. Why, Lord, did I study that? Why did I go there? Why, Lord, did you not stop me making that big mistake? Why, Lord, did you allow me to be subject to unwarranted criticism? Why, Lord, have you let me experience suffering like that? Later I can occasionally see why. Some of the uncomfortable passages of life have shaped and moulded me far more than the comfortable ones. But even if I can't see them 'working together for good' yet, I know that one day they will. As Paul assured the Philippians, 'he who began a good work in you will carry it on to completion until the day of Christ Jesus' (Philippians 1:6).

All this is for 'good'. Ah, that's the crucial word. What does 'good' mean? The good Paul refers to is not the superficial and material good we often seek in our transient short-term life but the ultimate, true good of our eternal life. As the New Testament scholar C.E.B. Cranfield wrote, 'Paul does not mean all things serve the comfort or convenience or worldly interest of the believers: it is obvious they do not. What he means is they "assist our salvation".'[69] They produce a more mature faith, a more certain hope, and a greater closeness to God than we might otherwise have had and that leads us to become like Jesus, as verse 29 explains.

There is perhaps no greater biblical illustration of this truth than Joseph, although he is far from unique. A precocious youth with a sense of destiny, he was detested by his brothers, who sold him into slavery as soon as the opportunity presented itself. In Egypt he began to rebuild his life and gain a position of trust and responsibility, only for it to be dashed to pieces by an evil temptress whose overtures he resisted. He languished forgotten in prison for over two years, except by God who 'was with him' in the jail (Genesis 39:21). During those years, he must often have thought his life was an insignificant waste. But he was remarkably 'rediscovered' after that and appointed 'ruler of Egypt' with authority second only to Pharaoh himself. The pit of slavery and the dungeon of Egypt had not proved worthless mistakes, but were all part of God 'working together' in his life to equip him and fit him for his strategic role. He said exactly that when reunited with his estranged brothers: 'You intended to harm me, but God intended it for good...' (50:20).

2. How?

The popular musical about Joseph comes nowhere near explaining the story. This is not about the power of positive thinking, nor about the way 'any dream will do', but, as the biblical account labours to stress, about the active planning, intervention and sovereignty of God who works in all things for good.

Without God's role in this verse,[70] Paul's saying becomes just another bit of popular mythology that was common in the ancient world. Today it might be based on 'evolutionary optimism'[71] or an even shakier foundation. 'It will all work out.' 'It's fate.' 'It will be OK.' 'Think positively.' 'Let's pin our hope on progress.' But that would be far from Paul's intention. His purpose is to celebrate God's wise superintendence over our lives.

Who is this God? None other than the God who is creator, who brought order out of chaos, light out of darkness, life out of emptiness, something out of nothing. What he did at the beginning on a cosmic scale, he does still on a personal scale.

Who is this God? None other than the God who is our Father, and who always intends and plans good for us and who, unlike human fathers, never fails or gets it wrong.

Who is this God? None other than the God who is sovereign, whose will cannot be thwarted and whose power cannot be defeated. He is the God who rolled back the stone that sealed the tomb of Jesus, defeating the strongest power on earth, that of death. No human can overcome this final enemy, but God has done so. He is the sovereign for whom there are no surprises, who can never be caught out, whom humans cannot frustrate and who will never encounter anyone more powerful than he is.

Good comes about in our lives by God's design and purpose.

3. Who?

Far from being a general piece of wishful thinking that applies to everyone, this verse of hope-filled wisdom is targeted at a specific audience. God works in all things 'for the good of those who love him'. To love God was something Israel had been taught to do from its earliest days. The language of love was enshrined in the third of the ten commandments which forbade idolatry (Exodus 20:6; Deuteronomy 5:10), and was at the heart of the covenant between the people of Israel and their faithful God (Deuteronomy 7:9). They knew it was the greatest commandment and at the root of all the law and the prophets (Matthew 22:34–40). They knew they were to 'love the Lord your God with all your heart and with all your soul and with all your strength' (Deuteronomy 6:5), long before Jesus reminded them of it in talking with the 'expert in the law' who provoked the story of the Good Samaritan (Luke 10:27). Love was the only proper response Israel could offer to God's grace and compassion. Israel's relationship with God was never meant to be one of fearsome subservience or dutiful obedience but one bathed in love.

Such talk might have been common in the worship of Israel but it was not to be heard in the Gentile world. Roman and Greek gods were served, worshipped, appeased and even manipulated, but not loved. Love speaks of an active, ongoing personal relationship between the deity and his subjects and so of a quality of relationship unknown among other religious people.

Paul does not limit God's intentional activity here to 'those who love him' to make his readers insecure. He was not intending to turn what is a statement of assurance into a question of interrogation. We regularly turn the statements of scripture into questions. Jesus says, 'You *are* the salt of the earth', whereas preachers today say, 'Are you the salt of the earth?' Paul says Jesus rose from the dead so has the pre-eminence in everything, whereas preachers ask, 'Does he have the pre-eminence in your life?' As if we could make him any more pre-eminent than he already is! Such translations of statements into questions or exhortations are well meant, but misguided. Scripture often sets out our identity in Christ as the basis on which we build fruitful Christian lives, rather than laying down a standard we have to achieve before God works in and through us. That's what's happening here.

Paul is not asking the Romans to examine themselves to see whether they love God enough to deserve his working things out for them. Of course, there is a place to examine the genuineness of one's love and faith. But that's not Paul's point in Romans 8:28, where he is simply laying down the truth that this is what God does. It's in his nature to work things out for the good of all those whose basic commitment in life revolves around loving God. His divine orchestration of our lives is not for the good of a select class of Christians who have reached a certain fervour, intensity or degree in their love for him, but for all who love him.

When we have this love for God it will lead us to interpret the experiences of life in a particular way. The difficult experiences of life can either drive us to trust God more or drive us away from him. I was leading an Agnostics Anonymous group in a pub some years ago where I would briefly introduce a topic and then open it up for discussion to be shot at. This particular evening the topic was 'Why does a good God allow suffering?' As soon as I finished one man jumped in to say he couldn't believe in God because he'd been a soldier in Northern Ireland and he and his mates had suffered horrific injuries when a troop carrier in which they were travelling had been blown up. Immediately afterwards, a young man, whom I recognised but hardly knew since he had only just started coming to the church where I was pastor, gave his testimony and described how he had been in the same situation when serving in Northern Ireland and it had driven him more fully into the arms of God. No one pretends such responses are easy or automatic. But there is a basic level of trust on which the one who loves God builds, which is absent from the one who does not love God or who has no real relationship with him.

Alister Begg tells the story of 'a sailor on the south coast of England who told his chaplain, "Chaplain, you don't understand. You're telling us to walk the straight and narrow path. But you don't realise the temptations we face, the way we're blown and tossed about. We can't really be blamed for what happens to us." The chaplain drew the sailor's attention to the water, where two sailboats were moving along with their sails flapping in the wind. One was heading west, the other east. The chaplain said, "One boat goes east, one boat goes west. By the self-same winds that blow. It's the set of their sails and not the gales, that determine which way they go."'[72]

When our sails are set to loving God, we'll go in the direction of serving his purposes.

4. Why?

Paul then, as it were, examines the other side of the same coin. Having examined our side—we love God—he now examines God's side—he has called us. As he is sovereign Lord, his call is more of a summons than an invitation[73] and, in line with that, the reason for his summons is so that he can achieve his purpose in our lives.

What is that purpose? In a nutshell it is our salvation. It is his 'eternal purpose of mercy'.[74] The achievement of that purpose develops through a number of steps (see Romans 8:29–30), each of which leads to another, but from the bottom step to the top it is God who takes the initiative and empowers us to ascend the ladder.

- Step 1, 'foreknew': God knew us intimately and personally before hand. To 'know' in Hebrew is about relationships, not about gathering information.
- Step 2, 'predestined': God elected us for a particular outcome.
- Step 3, 'called': God summoned us to serve his purposes.
- Step 4, 'justified': God set us in a right standing with him, overcoming any accusations against us. This has been the subject of Romans 4—7.
- Step 5, 'glorified': God intends us to share his glory in the new creation. So certain is this glory that Paul writes about it as if it has already happened, using the past tense. Here is the completion of the process.

His purpose, then, terminates in our sharing in his glory, which is the subject of our next and final chapter. But we must not pass on too hurriedly, since into the middle of these steps Paul slips something of vital importance about the purpose of our calling. It is not only a calling to glory but a calling 'to be conformed to the image of his

Son' (Romans 8:29). Salvation is not a status badge we can wave in a superior manner in the face of others who have not gained it. It is a call to transformation. Glory may complete the process but it begins here and now. As F.F. Bruce put it, using the word 'sanctification' for our progressive holiness, 'the difference between sanctification and glory is one of degree only, not one of kind. Sanctification is glory begun; glory is sanctification complete.'[75]

God's purpose for us is that we progressively change until we become the spitting image of Christ (without the caricatures which were involved in the TV programme of that name). Ambitions, attitudes and actions conform more to those Christ exhibited than to our natural reactions to things. Emotions come more and more under his control. Speech becomes filled with his grace. Stubborn wills are humbled and become more surrendered to him. Characters become Christlike. It is another way of expressing the calling that we examined in chapter 3: 'We are called into fellowship with his Son.' That's God's grand design for us.

Everything in our lives is governed by the purpose of God for us. None of it is arbitrary. The tennis coach may subject his players to punishing exercise regimes and ice baths, not because he is cruel but to bring out the absolute best of which each player is capable so that they can win the tournament. The football manager may impose a strict training schedule on his team and insist on no alcohol and early to bed before a crunch match, not to be awkward but to enable them to win the cup. God permits the good and the bad to happen in our lives, and is never frustrated by any of it, but works in all things to achieve his purpose of Christlikeness in us and glory for us.

5. When?

This work of God is neither a quick fix nor short-term. Glory is yet to come, even if Paul's utter confidence in it makes him use the past tense as if it has already happened. We won't necessarily see it all make sense next week and we're likely to struggle to 'be conformed to the image of his Son' until our dying day. If you are an impatient character, as I am, you want all this to have happened yesterday. Paul, however, stands back from our little lives and paints them on a much greater canvas. Our struggles, pain, failures and successes are trivial in view of the wider context. As John Stott wrote, Paul's 'great Spirit-directed mind now sweeps over the whole counsel of God from an eternity that is past to an eternity that is yet to come...'[76] It is God's great 'unchangeable, irresistible and invincible purpose' that is the eternal security of those who are called.[77]

Key lesson
Trust in God at all times, even when little sense can be made of what's happening in your life. He will bring your ultimate good out of it.

Questions
1. Revisit the life of Joseph (Genesis 37—50). How was his life shaped by the tough experiences he endured? Can you see the purposes of God being served through it all?
2. Trace difficult times in your own life. Did they drive you towards God or away from him? Can you begin to see God's wisdom in permitting them or are you still holding on and waiting for the day when they will make sense?
3. Do you see God as actively arranging your life, or merely responding to what happens, or not involved at all? Why do you think this?
4. What, in your own words, would you say are God's purposes for you?

12

Called to glory

Live lives worthy of God, who calls you into his kingdom and glory.
1 THESSALONIANS 2:12

He called you to this through our gospel, that you might share in the glory of our Lord Jesus Christ.
2 THESSALONIANS 2:14

And the God of all grace, who called you to his eternal glory in Christ, after you have suffered a little while, will himself restore you and make you strong, firm and steadfast.
1 PETER 5:10

'We're here at last,' said our guide. It had been a long and arduous journey. We had flown across the world, changing planes and hanging around one airport for several hours en route. The exotic attraction of airports I'd felt in earlier days with their eye-popping displays and seductive merchandise had long since faded. Once we had arrived at our destination airport, the journey was anything but over. A six-hour drive with an armed guard over rough terrain, well beyond any hint of civilisation, in a Jeep whose shock absorbers felt as if they had seen better days, lay ahead. The final approach to our home for the next couple of weeks was a mud bath. For all our exhaustion, how glad we were to learn that we had arrived!

The sight that greeted us didn't look promising. It was a refugee camp crammed full of those who were nothing but inconvenient refuse in the eyes of the powerful nations around. Yet, what glory we found in the camp as we met the Christians who lived there and joined in worship and teaching the Bible with them. What hope, what joy, what smiles, what love for God they showed. They put the miserable, materially rich but spiritually poor Western church to shame. They had been called to glory and were determined to begin to experience it, even if only a tiny bit, already in this dumping ground of the earth.

Glory is the final destination of the believer in Jesus Christ. It is to glory we are ultimately called, a glory we will no longer have to anticipate but one we will actually experience.

The God of glory

'Glory' is one of those words that occurs frequently in the Bible but seems to belong to the pious trappings of a past age rather than the contemporary world. Glory feels like the gold and crimson niceness of a geriatric House of Lords, or reminds us of old black floppy Bibles printed on very thin Indian paper, edged in gold; nice but not at the cutting edge of things. What is glory? Originally the word was connected with the weight of something, and so related to its value and worth. From that, its use developed and it came to mean people's opinion of someone and hence their worth or reputation. It was only a short step from that to it meaning 'visible splendour'.[78]

God's glory

The glory of God runs through the Bible from Genesis to Revelation. First seen in the creation of Adam and Eve in God's own image, that glory was soon tarnished by sin (Genesis 1:27; Psalm 8:5). After that, the manifestation of God's glory really begins with Moses. He encountered it and Israel witnessed it as 'a consuming fire' on Mount Sinai (Exodus 24:15–17). When Moses wanted to see more of it, God told him that since he was only a human being he would be unable to bear the sight of it. So, protected in a shelter, he was permitted merely to glimpse the back of God's glory as God passed by (Exodus 33:18–23). God's glory was concealed in cloud and fire as he descended again on Sinai and as he later took up his place in the tabernacle, and later the temple

(Exodus 34:5–7; 40:34–35; 1 Kings 8:11; 2 Chronicles 5:13–14; 7:1–3).

It was in the temple that a young Isaiah was overwhelmed by a vision of God's glory (Isaiah 6:1–13). He saw God as awesome in majesty, transcendent in power, magnificent in appearance and altogether pure in his being. As a result Isaiah was called to be a prophet calling Israel to repentance. Alas, when they did not heed his words and when God's patience ran out because they had so fully trashed their covenant with him, the people of Israel were sent into exile in Babylon. Ezekiel described that awful moment of Israel's downfall with these words: 'then the glory of the Lord departed' from the temple in Jerusalem (Ezekiel 10:18). After around 70 years, Israel was permitted to return to rebuild the land. Again it was to the language of God's glory they resorted to describe their experience. Isaiah celebrated the return as an act of God's glory (Isaiah 35:2; 40:5; 60:1–2), while Ezekiel envisaged God's glory re-entering the new temple, as surely as it had departed from the old one (Ezekiel 43:4–5).

With the coming of Jesus the revelation of God's glory takes on a new complexion. His glory is located in the person of his Son, rather than the building of the temple. God's awesome glory was too powerful to encounter face to face, as Moses learned, just as high-voltage electrical energy is too powerful to be anything other than destructive to us, unless it is transformed to enter our homes and empower our gadgets safely. So Jesus transforms the invisible glory of God into visible humanity and enables us to access it. God's glory was largely hidden but nonetheless was unmistakably seen in Jesus, and seen not only when he was performing one of his powerful miracles, but throughout. It was a glory 'full of grace and truth' (John 1:14).

Ironically, it was the most shameful episode of his life, that of his trial and execution as a common criminal, that Jesus believed to be the greatest manifestation of his glory (John 12:23, 28; 13:31–32; 17:1–5). He went to his cross as a king goes to his throne. He wore the crown of thorns as a king wears the crown of state. The weakness of God was truly more powerful than all the strength men could muster. In embracing shame, God manifested more majesty than all the trappings of human royalty put together.

Beyond the shame, the God of Moses, Isaiah and Ezekiel remains the same. He is still 'a consuming fire' (Hebrews 12:29). He reigns in majesty now, receiving the glory, honour and power of his creatures (Revelation 4:1–11). And he is in the process of removing all the evil dross and impurity that defiles the world he has made, so that in due course his glorious kingdom may be visible to all and unchallenged by any (Revelation 19:11–21; 20:7–15).

God's grace

When Peter writes about our call to glory, however, it is not God's glory, but his grace, that is uppermost in his mind. The problem with glory is that it can be heard as an awesome and impersonal power that overwhelms all in its path. Nothing could be further from the truth as far as God is concerned. His glory would be deficient if it were not suffused with grace.

From the time God revealed himself to be a God of glory he also revealed himself to be a God of grace. When Moses climbed Sinai to receive the second set of tablets on which the ten commandments were carved, God's glory came down in a cloud, but the voice Moses heard from the cloud proclaimed that the Lord was 'the compassionate and gracious God, slow to anger, abounding in love and faithfulness, maintaining love to thousands, and forgiving wickedness, rebellion and sin' (Exodus 34:6–7).

It is not right to see God's glory and holiness as distinct from his grace and compassion, as if they were two parallel lines on a railway track that, however necessary each of them is to the other, never meet. Nor is it adequate to see them as two blades in a pair of scissors, which unless both are present would prove worthless. God's glory and grace are more like a major musical chord which consists of several notes that harmonise. One note alone is not enough. In a C major chord, C is the root note, but E and G are vital and integral elements of the chord. Glory and grace are integral to each other. Without grace, glory might be a mere exercise in power. Without glory, grace could be a mere act of sentimentality. Glory is tempered by grace. Grace is made real by glory. The glory of God is offended by sin. The grace of God forgives sin. The glory of God moves against sin and seeks to remove every destructive force in his creation. The grace of God moves towards the sinner, enabling a way of pardon, reconciliation and renewal, without detriment to God's holiness. But the distinctive contribution each note makes to the chord should not be overdrawn since it is precisely the combination of God's glory and his grace that leads to the cross where God gives himself in the person of his Son for the sin of the world. Glory and grace harmonise to save sinners.

Peter says that God is the God of *all* grace (1 Peter 5:10; see also 2 Corinthians 12:9; Ephesians 1:6–8; 1 Peter 1:2; James 4:6). The New Testament writers generally go out of their way to stress the sufficiency and even the abundance of God's grace, especially in situations where Christians are up against it and in need of comfort and strengthening. Peter's readers, as chapter 8 explained, were suffering, mostly for their faith, although sometimes unjustly, and in that context Peter assures them that God's grace is available to them. If he had been familiar with Paul's second letter to the Corinthians he might have quoted his dictum, forged on the anvil of his own suffering: 'My grace is sufficient for you, for my power is made perfect in weakness' (2 Corinthians 12:9). As the old saying goes, 'The will of God will never take you where the grace of God cannot keep you.' We may not always understand, but we can always trust to God's grace.

In the midst of our sufferings, Peter says, God will aid us in four ways. God himself will restore what is damaged, strengthen what is weak, make firm what is unstable, and make steadfast what is unreliable. These are not separate outcomes of God's grace but all of a piece, one phrase piled on top of another to make their effect more pronounced. Furthermore, this is not a new topic that Peter finally gets around to at the end of his letter, but a return to its beginning. In 1 Peter 1:5 he has described his readers as those 'who through faith are shielded by God's power until the coming of the salvation that is ready to be revealed in the last time'. Now he tells us some of the ways in which God keeps his people. Watchman Nee, a Chinese leader who knew his own share of suffering, once expressed concern at the 'distressing fact that some Christians can believe in God's saving power, but they cannot believe in His keeping power'.[79] God's grace has both saving and keeping power.

Moreover, God's grace has vindicating power. Shame may be their, and our, lot now, but glory will be their and our lot then. Oppressors will encounter God's displeasure as surely as Pharaoh did in Egypt. Believers will be revealed as sons and daughters of God and receive their reward for the suffering they have endured. Paul was right when he considered that 'our present sufferings are not worth comparing with the glory that will be revealed in us' when creation is renewed (Romans 8:18).

Sharing in the glory of Jesus Christ

There is another detail on which Peter and Paul agree when they speak of our call to glory, which is that our glory is 'in Christ'. Paul expresses it a little more fully: 'that you may share in the glory of our Lord Jesus Christ' (2 Thessalonians 2:14). The glory to which we are called is not something other than the glory that we find in Jesus but the same glory as we find in him.

In fact, it's not quite as neat as that suggests. The New Testament writers do not always demonstrate the concern for precision and analytical compartmentalisation that modern writers love. So, in the three texts which speak about our call to glory, in the first it is God who calls us, in the second it is the gospel that calls us, and in the third it is God who calls us in Christ. But there is no need to drive a wedge between these since God is always 'the God and Father of our Lord Jesus Christ', the gospel is always 'the gospel of God', and Jesus is always the Son of God. Despite this somewhat technical detour, it is clear that the main thrust not only of these verses but of teaching elsewhere is that our call to glory is a call to share in Christ's glory. How so?

The clue lies in the idea of inheritance. Most people inherit because they are children of the deceased. In contrast to previous generations where everything was left to the older son, the inheritance is now usually shared equally between the sons and daughters of the family. The same is true, says Paul to the Romans, of our eternal glory. 'Now if we are children, then we are heirs—heirs of God and co-heirs with Christ, if indeed we share in his sufferings in order that we may also share in his glory' (Romans 8:17).

Jesus is heir to the entire renewed cosmos, in which 'all things in heaven and on earth' will find unity under his control (Ephesians 1:10). Ours is the immense, mind-boggling privilege of being 'co-heirs' with him, and so of entering into our shared inheritance. That means sharing in its joys and its responsibilities. Our task in the new creation will be 'to reign for ever and ever' (Revelation 22:5). Does that mean we will sit on thrones and be waited on by flunkies who satisfy our every whim? No, a thousand times no. God commissioned Adam and Eve to 'reign' or 'rule' over the creation (Genesis 1:28–30) but, through their sin, they imperfectly fulfilled their calling. Our calling to glory is a calling to do in the new creation what Adam and Eve were commissioned to do in the original creation, but free from the possibility of its being spoiled by sin. The call to glory is not a call to idleness or to an eternal vacation, but to the eternal service of God in the recreated cosmos.

A family relationship

Our right to inherit glory is dependent on our being members of God's family, which makes us 'co-heirs with Christ'. We have no claim on God and his gift of future glory apart from that. We are qualified to inherit because Christ has made it possible for us to be born into God's family. He alone has the authority to grant us this relationship and status (John 1:12). In explaining this, John insists this doesn't come about naturally, because we're Jewish, or British, or American, or because we were brought up in a Christian home, were baptised as a baby or attended Sunday school as a child, or because we're Anglican, Methodist, Baptist, Presbyterian, Brethren or Pentecostal, or whatever. While some of these things may help (some may not!), something else is required which John can only describe in a variety of birth images as 'a new birth', being 'born of God', being 'born again', meaning 'born from above' or 'born of the Spirit' (John 1:13; 3:1–9). Such a birth occurs as people 'receive' Christ, by which he means believing in him, not as an act of mental assent but as an act of total trust. To believe in him is to become his disciple, to receive his forgiveness, to obey his teaching and to live, not occasionally or periodically but daily, with our lives revolving around his.

Some time ago I was taken to the airport in Denmark by a champion pole vaulter. I'd never talked to one before, so I was full of questions. What on earth possessed anyone to take up this sport? How did you get started in it? Was it exciting or scary? What technique was involved (not that I was thinking of taking it up, you understand)? Had the pole ever snapped on him? (It had!) Had he ever missed the mat and landed awkwardly? And so on. It struck me as he patiently answered my ignorant questions that pole vaulting is a great illustration of what the Bible means by faith. The athlete runs down the track, aiming to get the pole into the pocket at the end of it, so they can swing themselves high into the air and propel themselves over the bar. As they do so, they are staking their life on the pole, entrusting all their weight to it. If it doesn't work, there's no way out. Likewise, to have faith in Jesus is to stake one's whole life on him, to put one's whole weight on him, and to trust in the grace that flows from his cross. If he doesn't save us and take us to glory, there is no other option for us to rely on.

This faith makes Jesus Christ our brother and leads us to become sons and daughters of God. Consequently, the inheritance, which was his through his resurrection and entering into glory at his exaltation on Ascension Day, is one we share.

A suffering relationship

Before we run away with the thought of the riches that will come our way one day, though, Paul pulls us back and points out the condition which is incorporated into the will: 'if indeed we share in his sufferings in order that we may also share in his glory' (Romans 8:17). It's not a matter of signing the family register so we can stake our claim to our share of the inheritance in due course. The relationship is much deeper than that. To become a member of this family is to be joined to Christ, to be united to him, to participate in him. And since he was the Christ who suffered, we must suffer with him. We cannot pick and choose the bits of Christ we like to suit our convenience. We either have Christ crucified, and risen, or we don't have Christ.

Perhaps this is why, when the New Testament writers speak about the glory that is to come, they usually do so as an incentive to Christians who were suffering, as in the texts mentioned at the beginning of this chapter. In their current lives they were experiencing shame. They were ridiculed, socially ostracised, beaten and in other ways subjected to physical abuse. In a society that was acutely sensitive to shame, this was truly awful. But while shame might be their lot here, glory would be their lot in the new creation. What better encouragement could there be than knowing that being 'in Christ' might cost now but would be immensely rewarding in the future?

Eternal glory

What?

Earthly glory fades. Athletic records are broken. Great achievements win applause one year and are overtaken the next. Yesterday's victories are soon forgotten. Great honours tarnish with time. President Jimmy Carter understood this. During a subsequent American presidential election when his fellow-ex-Presidents were on the campaign trail, the journalists tracked him down to a building project where they found him, saw in hand, building homes for the poor. When he was asked if he didn't miss the heady atmosphere of the political battle, he smiled his famous smile and replied, 'Such is passing fame.' The man who had once been the most powerful man on earth, as the Americans like to claim, knew that none of the honours on earth ultimately counted for anything. Earthly glory is inevitably transient. But the glory we are called to in Christ is 'eternal'.

- It is eternal glory because it belongs to the new age when creation will be restored.
- It is eternal glory because all opposition to it will be overthrown and it will be secure for all time.
- It is eternal glory because it will be immune from decay and partake of God's own eternal nature.
- It is eternal glory because it is glory of great worth, especially when compared with the baubles and trinkets this world offers by way of reward.
- It is eternal glory because it is a gift from 'the glorious Father' himself (Ephesians 1:17).

When?

The early Christians were united in the belief that the day when we would enter this eternal glory was the day on which Jesus himself would return. Setting aside the question of what happens to those who die between now and then, their focus was on the momentous and cosmic changes which would take place on his return.

Hear what Jesus himself said:

> At that time people will see the Son of Man coming in clouds with great power and glory. And he will send his angels and gather his elect from the four winds, from the ends of the earth to the ends of the heavens.
>
> MARK 13:26–27

And again he said to his apostles:

> Truly I tell you, at the renewal of all things, when the Son of Man sits on his glorious throne, you who have followed me will also sit on twelve thrones, judging the twelve tribes of Israel.
> MATTHEW 19:28

Hear what Paul said:

> God is just: he will pay back trouble to those who trouble you and give relief to you who are troubled, and to us as well. This will happen when the Lord Jesus is revealed from heaven in blazing fire with powerful angels... [The disobedient] will be punished with everlasting destruction and shut out from the presence of the Lord and from the glory of his might on the day he comes to be glorified in his holy people and to be marvelled at among all those who have believed.
> 2 THESSALONIANS 1:6–7, 9–10

Hear what Peter said:

> Praise be to the God and Father of our Lord Jesus Christ! In his great mercy he has given us new birth into a living hope through the resurrection of Jesus Christ from the dead, and into an inheritance that can never perish, spoil or fade. This inheritance is kept in heaven for you, who through faith are shielded by God's power until the coming of the salvation that is ready to be revealed in the last time.
> 1 PETER 1:3–5

Until the return of Christ 'we wait for the blessed hope—the appearing of the glory of our great God and Saviour, Jesus Christ' (Titus 2:13).

The blessings of God in this life may be abundantly rich and yet, as the hymn writer Isaac Watts put it centuries ago, all that we experience is merely 'glory begun below'. The destination of our calling is not 'glory begun' but glory complete as we spend eternity in the presence of our God and his Son, Jesus Christ.

Key lesson
Keep your eye fixed on the destination and do not be thrown by the journey to it, which may sometimes be uncomfortable.

Questions
1. Many sense a tension between the God of glory and the God of grace. How do you reconcile them?
2. Do you look forward to the coming again of Jesus Christ as 'a blessed hope' or as a blessed interruption to your own ambitions and plans?
3. How do you envisage your life in the new creation? How might you occupy your time? How does the Bible inform your vision of the future?
4. Look back over the twelve callings we have reviewed. Which one or two were especially relevant to you?

Notes

1 Ken Costa, *God at Work: Living every day with purpose* (Alpha, 2013); Mark Greene, *Thank God It's Monday* (Scripture Union, 2001); and Os Guinness, *The Call: Finding and fulfilling the central purpose of your life* (Word, 1998).

2 J.A. Motyer, *The Richness of Christ: Studies in the letter to the Philippians* (Inter-Varsity Fellowship, 1966), p. 17.

3 Adapted and expanded from Thomas Manton, *An Exposition of the Epistle of Jude* (Banner of Truth Trust, 1958), p. 16.

4 Older translations used the word 'called' where the NIV uses the word 'invited'.

5 National Service was abolished in 1960 during the reign of Queen Elizabeth II. The reference here is to King George VI.

6 C.S. Lewis, *The Four Loves* (Collins Fontana, 1963), p. 7.

7 Richard Bauckham, *Jude, 2 Peter* (Word, 1983), p. 26.

8 Manton, *Jude*, p. 43.

9 Manton, *Jude*, pp. 52–53.

10 'Overcome' might be translated 'understood'. Either way, the word indicates that the light has been rejected by the very people whom it was designed to benefit.

11 Roger Hargreaves, *Mr Clever* (Egmont, 1978).

12 Martyn Lloyd Jones, *Darkness and Light: An exposition of Ephesians 4:17—5:15* (Banner of Truth Trust, 1982), p. 37.

13 Elizabeth Achtemeier, *Preaching from the Old Testament* (Westminster John Knox Press, 1989), p. 102.

14 Achtemeier, *Preaching from the Old Testament*, p. 102.

15 Clinton Arnold, *Ephesians*, Exegetical Commentary on the New Testament (Zondervan, 2010), p. 282.

16 In verse 12 he speaks of Gentiles as 'at one time separated from Christ'.

17 Tom Smail, *Once and for All: A confession of the cross* (Darton, Longman & Todd, 1998), p. 106.

18 The text was examined in the previous chapter.

19 'The Grosvenor Chapel' in *Betjeman on Faith: An anthology of his religious prose*, ed. Kevin Gardner (SPCK, 2011).

20 Guy King, *The Fellowship: An exposition of First John* (CLC, 1954).

21 Michael Walker, *The God of Our Journey* (Marshall Pickering, 1989), pp. 26–27.

22 Anthony C. Thiselton, *The First Epistle to the Corinthians*, New International Greek Testament Commentary (Eerdmans, 2000), p. 104.

23 Cited in Murray J. Harris, *Slave of Christ: A New Testament metaphor for total devotion to Christ* (Apollos, 1999), p. 37. The description of slavery in this paragraph is drawn from pp. 33–45.

24 Masculine language is used in reference to slave owners because in reality the overwhelming majority of owners were men.

25 Harris, *Slave of Christ*, pp. 114–115.

26 Harris, *Slave of Christ*, p. 137.

27 Methodist Covenant Service, *Methodist Service Book* (Methodist Publishing House, 1984), p. 180.

28 See further chapter 2.

29 Harris, *Slave of Christ*, p. 95.

30 Nelson Mandela, *Long Walk to Freedom: The autobiography of Nelson Mandela* (Little, Brown & Co., 1994), p. 613.

31 Paul explains all this in detail in Galatians 3:15—4:7 as well as Romans 4:1–25.

32 Hebrews 10:5–10 states this clearly.

33 Richard Layard, *Happiness: Lessons from a new science* (Penguin, 2005), pp. 72–73.

34 Mandela, *Long Walk to Freedom*, p. 617.

35 John Hartley, *Leviticus*, Word Biblical Commentary (Word, 1992), p. 312.

36 See further Derek Tidball, *The Message of Leviticus*, The Bible Speaks Today (BST) (IVP, 2005), and *The Message of Holiness*, BST (IVP, 2010).

37 A fuller exposition of this passage is found in the author's *The Message of Holiness*, pp. 159–171.

38 J.C. Ryle, *Holiness: Its nature, hindrance, difficulties and roots* (James Clark & Co., repr. 1950), p. 35.

39 *The Westminster Collection of Christian Quotations*, compiled by Martin Manser (Westminster John Knox Press, 2001), p. 345.

40 David Atkinson, *Peace in Our Time* (Eerdmans, 1985), p. 137.

41 Paul mentions thankfulness six times in this letter (1:12; 2:7; 3:15, 16, 17; 4:2). They may have been a grumpy lot and this may have contributed to their tensions and conflicts.

42 Joni Eareckson Tada and Steve Estes, *A Step Further: Growing closer to God through hurt and hardship* (Zondervan, 1978), pp. 36–37. Italics original.

43 I owe this section particularly to Joel B. Green, *I Peter*, The Two Horizons New Testament Commentary (Eerdmans, 2007), p. 226.

44 Elsewhere Paul effectively transforms the customary rights of a master over his slaves by reminding them that they have a Master in heaven, to whom they are accountable (Ephesians 6:9; Colossians 4:1). See also the letter to Philemon.

45 A judicious overview of 'Worldwide Persecution of Christians' is given on www.seekingtruth.co.uk.

46 Edmund P. Clowney, *The Message of 1 Peter*, BST (IVP, 1988), p. 217.

47 Cited in Paul Mallard, *Invest Your Suffering: Unexpected intimacy with a loving God* (IVP, 2013), p. 21.

48 Mallard, *Invest Your Suffering*, pp. 125–126.

49 Paul uses the same idea in Colossians 1:24.

50 Green, *1 Peter*, p. 40.

51 Peter L. Berger, *A Rumour of Angels* (Pelican, 1971), p. 79.

52 'Profile: J.I. Packer', *Christianity* (February 2016), p. 35.

53 This is all explored more fully in chapter 7.

54 For more on this see chapter 5.

55 Andrew Fuller, 'Circular Letter to the Church of the Northampton Association' (1782). Italics original.

56 Note the city clerk's comments about the Christians, that 'they have neither robbed temples nor blasphemed our goddess' (v. 37). Perhaps this is a wise pattern for evangelism in multifaith areas.

57 Attributed to Søren Kierkegaard's *Fear and Trembling* (1843), although I have been unable to identity the exact quote from this book.

58 Jürgen Moltmann, *Theology of Hope*, trans. J.W. Leitch (SCM, 1967), p. 20.

59 The story is told in Paul Scott Wilson, *The Four Pages of the Sermon* (Abingdon, 1999), p. 225. I wish I could vouch for the veracity of this story, but I use it more as a preachers' parable than an actual happening.

60 I cannot now trace the source of this story, which was told of Cuthbert Bardsley, who became Bishop of Coventry. It is not included in Donald Coggan's biography of him.

61 Those who wish to explore this further should read Tom Wright, *Surprised by Hope* (SPCK, 2007), or J. Richard Middleton, *A New Heaven and a New Earth: Reclaiming biblical eschatology* (Baker Academic, 2014). More briefly I set out the texts in *The Voices of the New Testament: A conversational approach to the message of good news* (IVP, 2016), pp. 248–250.

62 C.S. Lewis, *Letters to Malcolm Chiefly on Prayer* (Geoffrey Bles, 1964), p. 122.

63 Wright, *Surprised by Hope*, p. 164.

64 Moltmann, *Theology of Hope*, p. 21.

65 Letter to Diognetus, chapter 5. The Letter is actually anonymous but frequently ascribed to one Mathetes, which means 'disciple'. The identity of Diognetus is also unknown but since he is addressed in the opening words as 'my lord' it is assumed he was a high-ranking pagan. This translation is found at www.vatican.va.

66 John Bunyan's *The Pilgrim's Progress* was first published in 1678.

67 Rudyard Kipling referred to six questions—what, why, when, how, where and who—in his *Just So Stories* (1902). I use five of these in what follows.

68 The NIV translation has lost the element of 'together', but Paul seems deliberately to use the word *sunergei*, with the prefix *sun* meaning 'together'.

69 C.E.B. Cranfield, *The Epistle to the Romans*, International Critical Commentary (T & T Clark, 1975), vol. 1, p. 428.

70 Some ancient manuscripts make God the subject of the sentence, while the majority leave his role as implicit, but no less real.

71 Leon Morris, citing C.H. Dodd, *The Epistle to the Romans* (Eerdmans, 1988), p. 331.

72 Alister Begg, *The Hand of God: Finding his care in all circumstances* (Moody Press, 1999), p. 73.

73 Douglas Moo, *The Epistle to the Romans*, New International Commentary on the New Testament (Eerdmans, 1996), p. 530.

74 Cranfield, *Romans*, p. 431.

75 F.F. Bruce, *The Epistle of Paul to the Romans*, Tyndale New Testament Commentaries (Tyndale Press, 1963), p. 178.

76 John R.W. Stott, *Men Made New* (IVP, 1966), p. 100.

77 Stott, *Men Made New*, p. 100.

78 The phrase is taken from Richard Bauckham, *Gospel of Glory: Major themes in Johannine theology* (Baker Academic, 2015), p. 44.

79 Watchman Nee, *God's Keeping Power* (Living Stream Ministry, 1993), p. 1.

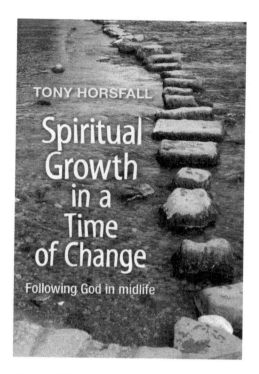

Midlife—our 40s and 50s—can be some of the most important years of our lives in spiritual terms. They are also times of change, which can include turbulent emotional transitions as we encounter a range of challenging personal issues. Tony Horsfall not only addresses a number of such issues—from facing up to the past to renegotiating relationships—but explores how to navigate a spiritual journey through these years, leading to deeper faith and a closer walk with God.

Spiritual Growth in a Time of Change
Following God in midlife
Tony Horsfall
978 0 85746 435 4 £7.99

brfonline.org.uk

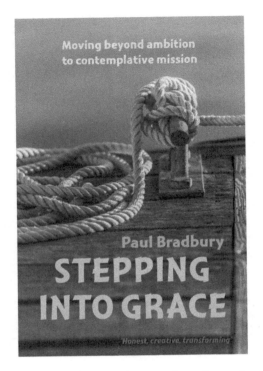

Moving beyond ambition
to contemplative mission

Paul Bradbury

STEPPING
INTO GRACE

Honest, creative, transforming

Journey with the prophet Jonah to explore the major themes of ambition, vocation, spirituality, mission, leadership and personal growth. Written by a fellow pioneer missionary, *Stepping into Grace* finds powerful connections between the call and mission of Jonah and the mission context of our own time. This unique journey takes us to a place of grace where the work of God in shaping who we are finds space alongside what we feel called to do.

Stepping into Grace
Moving beyond ambition to contemplative mission
Paul Bradbury
978 0 85746 523 8 £7.99

brfonline.org.uk

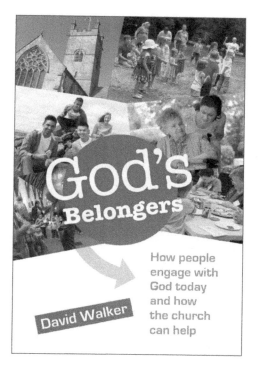

How people
engage with
God today
and how
the church
can help

David Walker

God's Belongers should transform our thinking about what it means to belong to Church. Uniquely, David Walker replaces the old and worn division between 'members' and 'non-members' with a four-fold model of belonging: through relationship, through place, through events and through activities. Based on extensive practical research, the author shows how 'belonging' can encompass a far wider group of people than those who attend weekly services. This opens up creative opportunities for mission in today's world.

God's Belongers
How people engage with God today and how the church can help
David Walker
978 0 85746 467 5 £8.99

brfonline.org.uk

Explore the freeing, life-changing nature of forgiveness...

As we move from Ash Wednesday to Easter Day, daily reflections and prayers help us to experience the living power of the cross of Christ through biblical and modern-day stories of wrongdoing and forgiveness. Our journey through Lent will deepen our response to God's love and, as we allow the Holy Spirit to do his work, we will see spiritual transformation in our lives today.

The Living Cross
Exploring God's gift of forgiveness and new life
Amy Boucher Pye
978 0 85746 512 2 £8.99

brfonline.org.uk

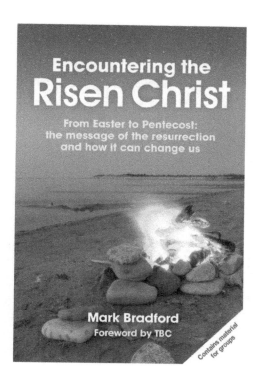

Encountering the
Risen Christ

From Easter to Pentecost:
the message of the resurrection
and how it can change us

Mark Bradford
Foreword by TBC

Contains material for groups

The resurrection of Jesus is at the heart of the Christian faith, but we tend to celebrate Easter as a day rather than a season. If we turn to the New Testament, we find some of the most profound and personal encounters with Christ in the post-Easter narratives. The risen Jesus comes to his disciples in their brokenness and calls them to a future filled with joy, forgiveness and new beginnings.

Encountering the Risen Christ
From Easter to Pentecost: the message of the resurrection and how it can change us
Mark Bradford
978 0 85746 428 6 £7.99

brfonline.org.uk

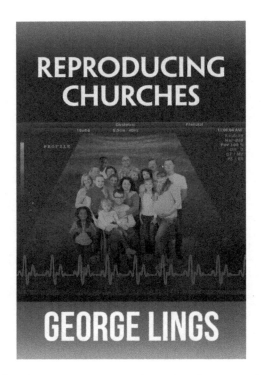

A ground-breaking perspective on how churches reproduce. In an original and exciting theological move, senior authority on fresh expressions of Church and church planting George Lings suggests that we look at Church differently. Based on extensive research, Lings argues that the Church has a calling and capacity to reproduce which is inherent in what Church is, rather than as its function. This seminal and inspiring work will inform and re-energise Church leaders for the task in hand in this generation and beyond.

Reproducing Churches

George Lings

978 0 85746 464 4 £12.99

brfonline.org.uk

In a series of pithy, poignant and profound readings, this book explores the intersection of faith and life. Spotting parables in the everyday, it equips readers to explore whether they might be bumping into God without realising it. Heartening and often humorous, it applies biblical truth in a way that both fascinates and liberates.

Could this be God?
Bumping into God in the everyday
Brian Harris
978 0 85746 500 9 £8.99

brfonline.org.uk

Transforming
lives and communities

Christian growth and understanding of the Bible

Resourcing individuals, groups and leaders in churches for their own spiritual journey and for their ministry

Church outreach in the local community

Offering three programmes that churches are embracing to great effect as they seek to engage with their local communities and transform lives

Teaching Christianity in primary schools

Working with children and teachers to explore Christianity creatively and confidently

Children's and family ministry

Working with churches and families to explore Christianity creatively and bring the Bible alive

Visit **brf.org.uk** for more information on BRF's work
Review this book on Twitter using **#BRFconnect**

brf.org.uk

The Bible Reading Fellowship (BRF) is a Registered Charity (No. 233280)